Node.js By Example

Learn to use Node.js by creating a fully functional
social network

Krasimir Tsonev

PUBLISHING

BIRMINGHAM - MUMBAI

Node.js By Example

First published: May 2015

Production reference: 1190515

Published by Packt Publishing Ltd.
Livery Place
35 Livery Street
Birmingham B3 2PB, UK.

ISBN 978-1-78439-571-1

www.packtpub.com

Credits

Author
Krasimir Tsonev

Reviewers
Danny Allen
Alex (Shurf) Frenkel

Commissioning Editor
Akram Hussain

Acquisition Editors
Purav Motiwalla
Llewellyn Rozario

Content Development Editor
Shubhangi Dhamgaye

Technical Editor
Mrunal M. Chavan

Copy Editor
Vedangi Narvekar

Project Coordinator
Harshal Ved

Proofreaders
Stephen Copestake
Safis Editing

Indexer
Priya Sane

Production Coordinator
Shantanu N. Zagade

Cover Work
Shantanu N. Zagade

About the Author

Krasimir Tsonev is a coder with over 10 years of experience in web development. The author of *Node.js Blueprints, Packt Publishing*, he works with a strong focus on quality and usability. Krasimir is interested in delivering cutting-edge applications. He enjoys working in the software industry and has a passion for creating and discovering new and effective digital experiences. Right now, he is working with technologies such as HTML5/CSS3, JavaScript, PHP, and Node.js, but he originally started out as a graphic designer. Later, being a Flash developer, he spent several years using ActionScript3 and frameworks such as RobotLegs. After that, as a freelancer, he continued to deliver full-stack web services for his clients, taking care of the graphic design and frontend and backend programming. Right now, with the rise of mobile application development, Krasimir is enthusiastic about working on responsive applications that target various devices. He currently lives and works in Bulgaria. He graduated from the Technical University of Varna with both a bachelor's and a master's degree in computer science. He loves blogging, writing books, and giving talks on the latest trends in web development.

He has authored *Node.js Blueprints, Packt Publishing* (`https://www.packtpub.com/web-development/nodejs-blueprints`).

I want to thank my family, who supported me in the last several months.

About the Reviewers

Danny Allen is a full-stack web developer who focuses on usability, user experience, localization, and accessibility issues as the founder and director of the international user experience development consultancy Wonderscore Ltd.

Skilled in a wide range of backend and frontend technologies including Python, Django, JavaScript, Node.js, as well as HTML5/CSS3, his recent work has involved the design and implementation of e-learning and government projects in the United Kingdom.

His portfolio and contact details can be found at `http://dannya.uk`.

Alex (Shurf) Frenkel has worked in the field of web application development since 1998 (the beginning of PHP 3.X) and has extensive experience in system analysis and project management. Alex is a PHP 5.3 Zend Certified Engineer and is considered to be one of the most prominent LAMP developers in Israel. He is also a food blogger at `http://www.foodstuff.guru`.

In the past, Alex was the CTO of ReutNet, one of the leading Israeli web technology-based companies. He also worked as the CEO/CTO of OpenIview LTD—a company built around the innovative idea of breaching the IBM mainframe business with PHP applications. He was also the CTO and the chief architect of a start-up, GBooking. He also provided expert consulting services to different companies in various aspects of web-related technology.

Frenkel-Online is a project-based company that works with a number of professional freelance consultants in Israel and abroad. Currently, their permanent staff comprises several consultants in Israel and abroad for the company's PHP projects and a number of specialists in other programming languages for the rest of the projects.

Foodstuff.Guru is a pet project that brings not only high-style food, but also every day food to the Web that can be reviewed by people for people. The blog is multilingual and you can visit it at `http://www.foodstuff.guru`.

www.PacktPub.com

Support files, eBooks, discount offers, and more

For support files and downloads related to your book, please visit www.PacktPub.com.

Did you know that Packt offers eBook versions of every book published, with PDF and ePub files available? You can upgrade to the eBook version at www.PacktPub.com and as a print book customer, you are entitled to a discount on the eBook copy. Get in touch with us at service@packtpub.com for more details.

At www.PacktPub.com, you can also read a collection of free technical articles, sign up for a range of free newsletters and receive exclusive discounts and offers on Packt books and eBooks.

https://www2.packtpub.com/books/subscription/packtlib

Do you need instant solutions to your IT questions? PacktLib is Packt's online digital book library. Here, you can search, access, and read Packt's entire library of books.

Why subscribe?

- Fully searchable across every book published by Packt
- Copy and paste, print, and bookmark content
- On demand and accessible via a web browser

Free access for Packt account holders

If you have an account with Packt at www.PacktPub.com, you can use this to access PacktLib today and view 9 entirely free books. Simply use your login credentials for immediate access.

Table of Contents

Preface

Node.js is one of the present day's most popular technologies. Its growing community is known to produce a large number of modules every day. These modules can be used as building blocks for server-side applications. The fact that we use the same language (JavaScript) on both the server- and client-side make development fluent.

This book contains 11 chapters that contain a step-by-step guide to building a social network. Systems such as Facebook and Twitter are complex and challenging to develop. It is nice that we will learn what Node.js is capable of, but it is going to be much more interesting if we do that within a concrete context. The book covers basic phases such as the architecture and management of the assets' pipeline, and it discusses features such as users' friendship and real-time communication.

What this book covers

Chapter 1, *Node.js Fundamentals*, teaches the basics of Node.js, what stands behind the technology, and its module management system and package manager.

Chapter 2, *Architecting the Project*, reveals the power of build systems such as Gulp. Before starting with our social network, we will plan the project. We will talk about test-driven development and the Model-View-Controller pattern. The chapter will cover the Node.js modules that are needed to bootstrap the project.

Chapter 3, *Managing Assets*, covers the building of a web application. So, we have to deal with HTML, CSS, JavaScript, and images. In this chapter, we will go through the processes behind the serving of assets.

Chapter 4, *Developing the Model-View-Controller Layers*, is about the basic structure of our application. We will create classes for views, models, and controllers. In the next few chapters, we will use these classes as a base.

Chapter 5, Managing Users, is about implementing user registration, authorization, and profile management.

Chapter 6, Adding Friendship Capabilities, explains one of the main concepts behind modern social networks — friendship. The ability to find friends and follow their walls is an important part. This chapter is dedicated to the development of this relationship between users.

Chapter 7, Posting Content, states that the backbone of every social network is the content that users add into the system. In this chapter, we will implement the process of post making.

Chapter 8, Creating Pages and Events, states that providing the ability to users to create pages and events will make our social network more interesting. Users can add as many pages as they want. Other users will be able to join the newly created places in our network. We will also add code to collect statistics.

Chapter 9, Tagging, Sharing, and Liking, explains that besides posting and reviewing content, the users of a social network should be able to tag, share, and like posts. This chapter is dedicated to the development of these functions.

Chapter 10, Adding Real-time Chat, talks about the expectations of users, in today's world, to see everything that is happening right away. They want to communicate faster with each other. In this chapter, we will develop a real-time chat so that the users can send messages instantly.

Chapter 11, Testing the User Interface, explains that it is important to get the job done, but it is also important to cover working functionalities with tests. In this chapter, we will see how to test a user interface.

What you need for this book

The book is based on Node.js version 0.10.36. We will also use MongoDB (http://www.mongodb.org/) as a database and Ractive.js (http://www.ractivejs.org/) as a client-side framework.

Who this book is for

If you have knowledge of JavaScript and want to see how you can use it in the backend, this book is for you. It will lead you through the creation of a fairly complex social network. You will learn how to work with a database and create real-time communication channels.

Conventions

In this book, you will find a number of styles of text that distinguish between different kinds of information. Here are some examples of these styles, and an explanation of their meaning.

Code words in text, database table names, folder names, filenames, file extensions, pathnames, dummy URLs, user input, and Twitter handles are shown as follows: "If the Ractive component has a `friends` property, then we will render a list of users."

A block of code is set as follows:

```
<li class="right"><a on-click="goto:logout">Logout</a></li>
<li class="right"><a on-click="goto:profile">Profile</a></li>
<li class="right"><a on-click="goto:find-friends">Find
friends</a></li>
```

Any command-line input or output is written as follows:

```
sudo apt-get update
sudo apt-get install nodejs
sudo apt-get install npm
```

New terms and **important words** are shown in bold. Words that you see on the screen, in menus or dialog boxes for example, appear in the text like this: "It shows their name and a **Add as a friend** button."

 Tips and tricks appear like this.

Reader feedback

Feedback from our readers is always welcome. Let us know what you think about this book—what you liked or may have disliked. Reader feedback is important for us to develop titles that you really get the most out of.

To send us general feedback, simply send an e-mail to `feedback@packtpub.com`, and mention the book title via the subject of your message.

If there is a topic that you have expertise in and you are interested in either writing or contributing to a book, see our author guide on www.packtpub.com/authors.

Customer support

Now that you are the proud owner of a Packt book, we have a number of things to help you to get the most from your purchase.

Downloading the example code

You can download the example code files for all Packt books you have purchased from your account at http://www.packtpub.com. If you purchased this book elsewhere, you can visit http://www.packtpub.com/support and register to have the files e-mailed directly to you.

Errata

Although we have taken every care to ensure the accuracy of our content, mistakes do happen. If you find a mistake in one of our books—maybe a mistake in the text or the code—we would be grateful if you would report this to us. By doing so, you can save other readers from frustration and help us improve subsequent versions of this book. If you find any errata, please report them by visiting http://www.packtpub.com/submit-errata, selecting your book, clicking on the **errata submission form** link, and entering the details of your errata. Once your errata are verified, your submission will be accepted and the errata will be uploaded on our website, or added to any list of existing errata, under the Errata section of that title. Any existing errata can be viewed by selecting your title from http://www.packtpub.com/support.

Piracy

Piracy of copyright material on the Internet is an ongoing problem across all media. At Packt, we take the protection of our copyright and licenses very seriously. If you come across any illegal copies of our works, in any form, on the Internet, please provide us with the location address or website name immediately so that we can pursue a remedy.

Please contact us at copyright@packtpub.com with a link to the suspected pirated material.

We appreciate your help in protecting our authors, and our ability to bring you valuable content.

Questions

You can contact us at questions@packtpub.com if you are having a problem with any aspect of the book, and we will do our best to address it.

1
Node.js Fundamentals

Node.js is one of the most popular JavaScript-driven technologies nowadays. It was created in 2009 by Ryan Dahl and since then, the framework has evolved into a well-developed ecosystem. Its package manager is full of useful modules and developers around the world have started using Node.js in their production environments. In this chapter, we will learn about the following:

- Node.js building blocks
- The main capabilities of the environment
- The package management of Node.js

Understanding the Node.js architecture

Back in the days, Ryan was interested in developing network applications. He found out that most high performance servers followed similar concepts. Their architecture was similar to that of an event loop and they worked with nonblocking input/output operations. These operations would permit other processing activities to continue before an ongoing task could be finished. These characteristics are very important if we want to handle thousands of simultaneous requests.

Most of the servers written in Java or C use multithreading. They process every request in a new thread. Ryan decided to try something different—a single-threaded architecture. In other words, all the requests that come to the server are processed by a single thread. This may sound like a nonscalable solution, but Node.js is definitely scalable. We just have to run different Node.js processes and use a load balancer that distributes the requests between them.

Ryan needed something that is event-loop-based and which works fast. As he pointed out in one of his presentations, big companies such as Google, Apple, and Microsoft invest a lot of time in developing high performance JavaScript engines. They have become faster and faster every year. There, event-loop architecture is implemented. JavaScript has become really popular in recent years. The community and the hundreds of thousands of developers who are ready to contribute made Ryan think about using JavaScript. Here is a diagram of the Node.js architecture:

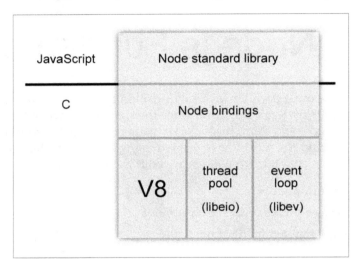

In general, Node.js is made up of three things:

- V8 is Google's JavaScript engine that is used in the Chrome web browser (`https://developers.google.com/v8/`)
- A thread pool is the part that handles the file input/output operations. All the blocking system calls are executed here (`http://software.schmorp.de/pkg/libeio.html`)
- The event loop library (`http://software.schmorp.de/pkg/libev.html`)

On top of these three blocks, we have several bindings that expose low-level interfaces. The rest of Node.js is written in JavaScript. Almost all the APIs that we see as built-in modules and which are present in the documentation, are written in JavaScript.

Installing Node.js

A fast and easy way to install Node.js is by visiting `https://nodejs.org/download/` and downloading the appropriate installer for your operating system. For OS X and Windows users, the installer provides a nice, easy-to-use interface. For developers that use Linux as an operating system, Node.js is available in the APT package manager. The following commands will set up Node.js and **Node Package Manager (NPM)**:

```
sudo apt-get update
sudo apt-get install nodejs
sudo apt-get install npm
```

Running Node.js server

Node.js is a command-line tool. After installing it, the `node` command will be available on our terminal. The `node` command accepts several arguments, but the most important one is the file that contains our JavaScript. Let's create a file called `server.js` and put the following code inside:

```
var http = require('http');
http.createServer(function (req, res) {
    res.writeHead(200, {'Content-Type': 'text/plain'});
    res.end('Hello World\n');
}).listen(9000, '127.0.0.1');
console.log('Server running at http://127.0.0.1:9000/');
```

Downloading the example code

You can download the example code files from your account at `http://www.packtpub.com` for all the Packt Publishing books that you have purchased. If you purchased this book elsewhere, you can visit `http://www.packtpub.com/support` and register to have the files e-mailed directly to you.

If you run `node ./server.js` in your console, you will have the Node.js server running. It listens for incoming requests at localhost (`127.0.0.1`) on port `9000`. The very first line of the preceding code requires the built-in `http` module. In Node.js, we have the `require` global function that provides the mechanism to use external modules. We will see how to define our own modules in a bit. After that, the scripts continue with the `createServer` and `listen` methods on the `http` module. In this case, the API of the module is designed in such a way that we can chain these two methods like in jQuery.

The first one (`createServer`) accepts a function that is also known as a callback, which is called every time a new request comes to the server. The second one makes the server listen.

The result that we will get in a browser is as follows:

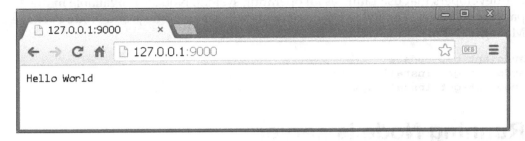

Defining and using modules

JavaScript as a language does not have mechanisms to define real classes. In fact, everything in JavaScript is an object. We normally inherit properties and functions from one object to another. Thankfully, Node.js adopts the concepts defined by **CommonJS**—a project that specifies an ecosystem for JavaScript.

We encapsulate logic in modules. Every module is defined in its own file. Let's illustrate how everything works with a simple example. Let's say that we have a module that represents this book and we save it in a file called `book.js`:

```
// book.js
exports.name = 'Node.js by example';
exports.read = function() {
    console.log('I am reading ' + exports.name);
}
```

We defined a public property and a public function. Now, we will use `require` to access them:

```
// script.js
var book = require('./book.js');
console.log('Name: ' + book.name);
book.read();
```

We will now create another file named `script.js`. To test our code, we will run `node ./script.js`. The result in the terminal looks like this:

```
$ node .\script.js
Name: Node.js by example
I'm reading Node.js by example
```

Along with `exports`, we also have `module.exports` available. There is a difference between the two. Look at the following pseudocode. It illustrates how Node.js constructs our modules:

```
var module = { exports: {} };
var exports = module.exports;
// our code
return module.exports;
```

So, in the end, `module.exports` is returned and this is what `require` produces. We should be careful because if at some point we apply a value directly to `exports` or `module.exports`, we may not receive what we need. Like at the end of the following snippet, we set a function as a value and that function is exposed to the outside world:

```
exports.name = 'Node.js by example';
exports.read = function() {
    console.log('Iam reading ' + exports.name);
}
module.exports = function() {  ... }
```

In this case, we do not have an access to `.name` and `.read`. If we try to execute `node ./script.js` again, we will get the following output:

```
book.read();
     ^
TypeError: undefined is not a function
```

To avoid such issues, we should stick to one of the two options — `exports` or `module.exports` — but make sure that we do not have both.

We should also keep in mind that by default, `require` caches the object that is returned. So, if we need two different instances, we should export a function. Here is a version of the `book` class that provides API methods to rate the books and that do not work properly:

```
// book.js
var ratePoints = 0;
exports.rate = function(points) {
    ratePoints = points;
}
exports.getPoints = function() {
    return ratePoints;
}
```

Let's create two instances and rate the books with different `points` value:

```
// script.js
var bookA = require('./book.js');
var bookB = require('./book.js');
bookA.rate(10);
bookB.rate(20);
console.log(bookA.getPoints(), bookB.getPoints());
```

The logical response should be 10 20, but we got 20 20. This is why it is a common practice to export a function that produces a different object every time:

```
// book.js
module.exports = function() {
    var ratePoints = 0;
    return {
        rate: function(points) {
            ratePoints = points;
        },
        getPoints: function() {
            return ratePoints;
        }
    }
}
```

Now, we should also have `require('./book.js')()` because `require` returns a function and not an object anymore.

Managing and distributing packages

Once we understand the idea of require and exports, we should start thinking about grouping our logic into building blocks. In the Node.js world, these blocks are called **modules** (or **packages**). One of the reasons behind the popularity of Node.js is its package management.

Node.js normally comes with two executables—node and npm. NPM is a command-line tool that downloads and uploads Node.js packages. The official site, https://npmjs.org/, acts as a central registry. When we create a package via the npm command, we store it there so that every other developer may use it.

Creating a module

Every module should live in its own directory, which also contains a metadata file called package.json. In this file, we have set at least two properties—name and version:

```
{
    "name": "my-awesome-nodejs-module",
    "version": "0.0.1"
}
```

We can place whatever code we like in the same directory. Once we publish the module to the NPM registry and someone installs it, he/she will get the same files. For example, let's add an index.js file so that we have two files in the package:

```
// index.js
console.log('Hello, this is my awesome Node.js module!');
```

Our module does only one thing—it displays a simple message to the console. Now, to upload the modules, we need to navigate to the directory containing the package.json file and execute npm publish. This is the result that we should see:

```
$ npm publish
npm http PUT https://registry.npmjs.org/my-awesome-nodejs-module
npm http 403 https://registry.npmjs.org/my-awesome-nodejs-module
npm http PUT https://registry.npmjs.org/my-awesome-nodejs-module
npm http 201 https://registry.npmjs.org/my-awesome-nodejs-module
+ my-awesome-nodejs-module@0.0.1
```

We are ready. Now our little module is listed in the Node.js package manager's site and everyone is able to download it.

Using modules

In general, there are three ways to use the modules that are already created. All three ways involve the package manager:

- We may install a specific module manually. Let's say that we have a folder called `project`. We open the folder and run the following:

```
npm install my-awesome-nodejs-module
```

The manager automatically downloads the latest version of the module and puts it in a folder called `node_modules`. If we want to use it, we do not need to reference the exact path. By default, Node.js checks the `node_modules` folder before requiring something. So, just `require('my-awesome-nodejs-module')` will be enough.

- The installation of modules globally is a common practice, especially if we talk about command-line tools made with Node.js. It has become an easy-to-use technology to develop such tools. The little module that we created is not made as a command-line program, but we can still install it globally by running the following code:

```
npm install my-awesome-nodejs-module -g
```

Note the `-g` flag at the end. This is how we tell the manager that we want this module to be a global one. When the process finishes, we do not have a `node_modules` directory. The `my-awesome-nodejs-module` folder is stored in another place on our system. To be able to use it, we have to add another property to `package.json`, but we'll talk more about this in the next section.

- The resolving of dependencies is one of the key features of the package manager of Node.js. Every module can have as many dependencies as you want. These dependences are nothing but other Node.js modules that were uploaded to the registry. All we have to do is list the needed packages in the `package.json` file:

```
{
    "name": "another-module",
    "version": "0.0.1",
    "dependencies": {
        "my-awesome-nodejs-module": "0.0.1"
    }
}
```

Now we don't have to specify the module explicitly and we can simply execute npm install to install our dependencies. The manager reads the package.json file and saves our module again in the node_modules directory. It is good to use this technique because we may add several dependencies and install them at once. It also makes our module transferable and self-documented. There is no need to explain to other programmers what our module is made up of.

Updating our module

Let's transform our module into a command-line tool. Once we do this, users will have a my-awesome-nodejs-module command available in their terminals. There are two changes in the package.json file that we have to make:

```
{
    "name": "my-awesome-nodejs-module",
    "version": "0.0.2",
    "bin": "index.js"
}
```

A new bin property is added. It points to the entry point of our application. We have a really simple example and only one file — index.js.

The other change that we have to make is to update the version property. In Node.js, the version of the module plays important role. If we look back, we will see that while describing dependencies in the package.json file, we pointed out the exact version. This ensures that in the future, we will get the same module with the same APIs. Every number from the version property means something. The package manager uses **Semantic Versioning 2.0.0** (http://semver.org/). Its format is *MAJOR.MINOR.PATCH*. So, we as developers should increment the following:

- MAJOR number if we make incompatible API changes
- MINOR number if we add new functions/features in a backwards-compatible manner
- PATCH number if we have bug fixes

Sometimes, we may see a version like 2.12.*. This means that the developer is interested in using the exact MAJOR and MINOR version, but he/she agrees that there may be bug fixes in the future. It's also possible to use values like >=1.2.7 to match any equal-or-greater version, for example, 1.2.7, 1.2.8, or 2.5.3.

We updated our `package.json` file. The next step is to send the changes to the registry. This could be done again with `npm publish` in the directory that holds the JSON file. The result will be similar. We will see the new **0.0.2** version number on the screen:

```
$ npm publish
npm http PUT  https://registry.npmjs.org/my-awesome-nodejs-module
npm http 201  https://registry.npmjs.org/my-awesome-nodejs-module
+ my-awesome-nodejs-module@0.0.2
```

Just after this, we may run `npm install my-awesome-nodejs-module -g` and the new version of the module will be installed on our machine. The difference is that now we have the `my-awesome-nodejs-module` command available and if you run it, it displays the message written in the `index.js` file:

```
$ my-awesome-nodejs-module
Hello, this is my awesome Node.js module!
```

Introducing built-in modules

Node.js is considered a technology that you can use to write backend applications. As such, we need to perform various tasks. Thankfully, we have a bunch of helpful built-in modules at our disposal.

Creating a server with the HTTP module

We already used the HTTP module. It's perhaps the most important one for web development because it starts a server that listens on a particular port:

```
var http = require('http');
http.createServer(function (req, res) {
    res.writeHead(200, {'Content-Type': 'text/plain'});
    res.end('Hello World\n');
}).listen(9000, '127.0.0.1');
console.log('Server running at http://127.0.0.1:9000/');
```

We have a `createServer` method that returns a new web server object. In most cases, we run the `listen` method. If needed, there is `close`, which stops the server from accepting new connections. The callback function that we pass always accepts the `request` (`req`) and `response` (`res`) objects. We can use the first one to retrieve information about incoming request, such as, GET or POST parameters.

Reading and writing to files

The module that is responsible for the read and write processes is called `fs` (it is derived from **filesystem**). Here is a simple example that illustrates how to write data to a file:

```
var fs = require('fs');
fs.writeFile('data.txt', 'Hello world!', function (err) {
    if(err) { throw err; }
    console.log('It is saved!');
});
```

Most of the API functions have synchronous versions. The preceding script could be written with `writeFileSync`, as follows:

```
fs.writeFileSync('data.txt', 'Hello world!');
```

However, the usage of the synchronous versions of the functions in this module blocks the event loop. This means that while operating with the filesystem, our JavaScript code is paused. Therefore, it is a best practice with Node to use asynchronous versions of methods wherever possible.

The reading of the file is almost the same. We should use the `readFile` method in the following way:

```
fs.readFile('data.txt', function(err, data) {
    if (err) throw err;
    console.log(data.toString());
});
```

Working with events

The observer design pattern is widely used in the world of JavaScript. This is where the objects in our system subscribe to the changes happening in other objects. Node.js has a built-in module to manage events. Here is a simple example:

```
var events = require('events');
var eventEmitter = new events.EventEmitter();
var somethingHappen = function() {
    console.log('Something happen!');
}
eventEmitter
.on('something-happen', somethingHappen)
.emit('something-happen');
```

The eventEmitter object is the object that we subscribed to. We did this with the help of the on method. The emit function fires the event and the somethingHappen handler is executed.

The events module provides the necessary functionality, but we need to use it in our own classes. Let's get the book idea from the previous section and make it work with events. Once someone rates the book, we will dispatch an event in the following manner:

```
// book.js
var util = require("util");
var events = require("events");
var Class = function() { };
util.inherits(Class, events.EventEmitter);
Class.prototype.ratePoints = 0;
Class.prototype.rate = function(points) {
    ratePoints = points;
    this.emit('rated');
};
Class.prototype.getPoints = function() {
    return ratePoints;
}
module.exports = Class;
```

We want to inherit the behavior of the EventEmitter object. The easiest way to achieve this in Node.js is by using the utility module (util) and its inherits method. The defined class could be used like this:

```
var BookClass = require('./book.js');
var book = new BookClass();
book.on('rated', function() {
    console.log('Rated with ' + book.getPoints());
});
book.rate(10);
```

We again used the on method to subscribe to the rated event. The book class displays that message once we set the points. The terminal then shows the **Rated with 10** text.

Managing child processes

There are some things that we can't do with Node.js. We need to use external programs for the same. The good news is that we can execute shell commands from within a Node.js script. For example, let's say that we want to list the files in the current directory. The file system APIs do provide methods for that, but it would be nice if we could get the output of the `ls` command:

```
// exec.js
var exec = require('child_process').exec;
exec('ls -l', function(error, stdout, stderr) {
    console.log('stdout: ' + stdout);
    console.log('stderr: ' + stderr);
    if (error !== null) {
        console.log('exec error: ' + error);
    }
});
```

The module that we used is called `child_process`. Its `exec` method accepts the desired command as a string and a callback. The `stdout` item is the output of the command. If we want to process the errors (if any), we may use the `error` object or the `stderr` buffer data. The preceding code produces the following screenshot:

```
$ node .\exec.js
stdout: total 1
-rw-r--r--    1 krasimir Administ      246 Sep 21 19:38 exec.js
-rw-r--r--    1 krasimir Administ        0 Sep 21 19:37 file.txt
```

Along with the `exec` method, we have `spawn`. It's a bit different and really interesting. Imagine that we have a command that not only does its job, but also outputs the result. For example, `git push` may take a few seconds and it may send messages to the console continuously. In such cases, `spawn` is a good variant because we get an access to a stream:

```
var spawn = require('child_process').spawn;
var command = spawn('git', ['push', 'origin', 'master']);
command.stdout.on('data', function (data) {
   console.log('stdout: ' + data);
});
command.stderr.on('data', function (data) {
   console.log('stderr: ' + data);
});
command.on('close', function (code) {
   console.log('child process exited with code ' + code);
});
```

Here, `stdout` and `stderr` are streams. They dispatch events and if we subscribe to these events, we will get the exact output of the command as it was produced. In the preceding example, we run `git push origin master` and sent the full command responses to the console.

Summary

Node.js is used by many companies nowadays. This proves that it is mature enough to work in a production environment. In this chapter, we saw what the fundamentals of this technology are. We covered some of the commonly used cases. In the next chapter, we will start with the basic architecture of our example application. It is not a trivial one. We are going to build our own social network.

2
Architecting the Project

Software development is a complex process. We can't just start writing some code and expect that we will reach our goal. We need to plan and define the base of our application. In other words, before you dive into actual scripting, you have to architect the project. In this chapter, we will cover the following:

- The basic layers of a Node.js application
- Using the task runner and building system
- Test-driven development
- The Model-View-Controller pattern
- The REST API concept

Introducing the basic layers of the application

If we plan to build a house, we will probably want to start with a very good base. We simply can't build the first and second floor if the base of the building is not solid.

However, with software, it is a bit different. We can start developing code without the existence of a good base. We call this **brute-force-driven development**. In this, we produce feature after feature without actually caring about the quality of our code. The result may work in the beginning, but in the long term, it consumes more time and probably money. It's well-known that software is nothing but building blocks placed on top of one another. If the lower layers of our program are poorly designed, then the whole solution will suffer because of this.

Let's think about our project—the social network that we want to build with Node.js. We start with a simple code like this one:

```
var http = require('http');
http.createServer(function (req, res) {
    res.writeHead(200, {'Content-Type': 'text/plain'});
    res.end('Hello World\n');
}).listen(1337, '127.0.0.1');
console.log('Server running at http://127.0.0.1:1337/');
```

The very first thing that you may notice is that you served a text to the user, but you probably wanted to serve file content. Node.js is similar to PHP. However, there is one fundamental difference. PHP needs a server that accepts the requests and passes them to the PHP interpreter. Then, the PHP code is processed and the response is delivered to the user again by the server. In the Node.js world, we don't have a separate external server. Node.js itself plays that role. It is up to the developer to handle the incoming requests and decide what to do with them.

If we take the preceding code and assume that we have page.html containing our basic HTML layout and the styles.css file holding the CSS styles, our next step will be as follows (check out the planning folder in the book's code samples):

```
var http = require('http');
var fs = require('fs');
http.createServer(function (req, res) {
    var content = '';
    var type = '';
    if(req.url === '/') {
        content = fs.readFileSync('./page.html');
        type = 'text/html';
    } else if(req.url === '/styles.css') {
        content = fs.readFileSync('./styles.css');
        type = 'text/css';
    }
    res.writeHead(200, {'Content-Type': type});
    res.end(content + '\n');
}).listen(1337, '127.0.0.1');
console.log('Server running at http://127.0.0.1:1337/');
```

We will check the incoming request's URL. If we just open http://127.0.0.1:1337/, we will receive the code of page.html as a response. If we have a <link> tag in the page.html file that requests style.css, the browser will fire a request for that too. The URL is different, but it is again caught by the if clause and then the proper content is served.

This is fine for now, but we will probably need to serve not two but many files. We do not want to describe all of them. So, this process should be optimized. The first layer of every Node.js server usually deals with routing. It parses the request's URL and decides what to do. If we need to deliver static files, then we will end up placing logic for that in an external module that finds the files, reads them, and sends a response with the proper content type. This can be the second layer of our architecture.

Along with the delivery of files, we will need to write some backend logic. This will be the third layer. Again, based on the URL, we will perform some actions related to the business logic, as follows:

```
var http = require('http');
var fs = require('fs');
http.createServer(function (req, res) {
    var content = '';
    var type = '';
    if(req.url === '/') {
        content = fs.readFileSync('./page.html');
        type = 'text/html';
    } else if(req.url === '/styles.css') {
        content = fs.readFileSync('./styles.css');
        type = 'text/css';
    } else if(req.url === '/api/user/new') {
            // Do actions like
        // reading POST parameters
        // storing the user into the database
        content = '{"success": true}';
        type = 'application/json';
    }
    res.writeHead(200, {'Content-Type': type});
    res.end(content + '\n');
}).listen(1337, '127.0.0.1');
console.log('Server running at http://127.0.0.1:1337/');
```

Note that we returned the JSON data. So now, our Node.js server acts as an API. We will talk about this at the end of this chapter.

The following diagram shows the three layers that we just talked about:

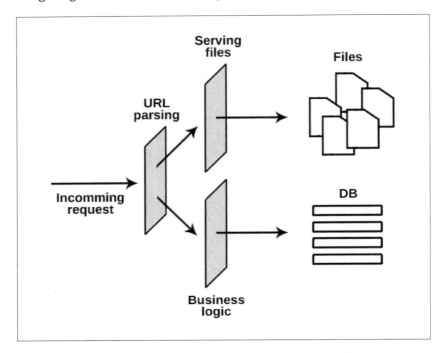

These will be the main layers of our application. In the chapters that follow, we will work on them. But before that, let's see what other work we have to do before we reach that point.

The task runner and building system

Along with the practice of running the Node.js server, there are other best practices pertaining to web development tasks that you can consider. We are building a web application. So, we have client-side JavaScript and CSS that has to be delivered in the best possible way. In other words, to increase the performance of our website, we need to merge all the JavaScript into a single file and compress it. The same is valid for the CSS style sheets. If you do this, the browser will make fewer requests to the server.

Node.js is a common tool for command-line utilities, except for when you want to run web servers. There are many modules available for the packaging and optimizing of assets. It is great that there are task runners and build systems that help you manage these processes.

Introducing Grunt

Grunt is one of the most popular task runners that are based on Node.js. It is available in the package manager registry and can be installed by using the following command:

```
npm install -g grunt-cli
```

Once we run that in the terminal, we will get a global `grunt` command at our disposal. We need to create a `Gruntfile.js` file in the root directory of the project, which is where we will define our tasks. By tasks, we mean actions such as concatenation and minification that we want to perform on specific files. Here is a simple `Gruntfile.js`:

```
module.exports = function(grunt) {
    grunt.initConfig({
        concat: {
            javascript: {
                src: 'src/**/*.js',
                dest: 'build/scripts.js'
            }
        }
    });
    grunt.loadNpmTasks('grunt-contrib-concat');
    grunt.registerTask('default', ['concat']);
}
```

In the first chapter of this book, we saw how one can define Node.js modules. The configuration needed by Grunt is just a simple module. We export a function that accepts a `grunt` object containing all the public API functions of the runner. In the `initConfig` block, we place our actions, and with `registerTask`, we combine actions and tasks. There should be at least one task that is defined with the name `default`. This is what Grunt runs if we don't pass additional parameters in the terminal.

There is one last function used in the preceding example— `loadNpmTasks`. The real power of Grunt is the fact that we have hundreds of plugins available. The `grunt` command is an interface that you can use to control these plugins when the real job is done. Since they are all registered in the Node.js package manager, we need to include them in the `package.json` file. For the preceding code, we need the following:

```
{
    "name": "GruntjsTest",
    "version": "0.0.1",
```

```
    "description": "GruntjsTest",
    "dependencies": {},
    "devDependencies": {
        "grunt-contrib-concat": "0.3.0"
    }
}
```

Let's continue by adding two other functionalities to our Grunt setup. Once we have the JavaScript concatenated, we will probably want a minified version of the compiled file; grunt-contrib-uglify is the module that does this job:

```
module.exports = function(grunt) {
    grunt.initConfig({
        concat: {
            javascript: {
                src: 'src/**/*.js',
                dest: 'build/scripts.js'
            }
        },
        uglify: {
            javascript: {
                files: {
                    'build/scripts.min.js': '<%= concat.javascript.dest %>'
                }
            }
        }
    });
    grunt.loadNpmTasks('grunt-contrib-concat');
    grunt.loadNpmTasks('grunt-contrib-uglify');
    grunt.registerTask('default', ['concat', 'uglify']);
}
```

We should mention that the uglify task should be run after the concat one because they depend on each other. There is also a shortcut — <%= concat.javascript.dest %>. We use such expressions to simplify the maintenance of the Gruntfile.js file.

We have Grunt tasks to process our JavaScript. However, it will be too annoying if we have to go back to the console and run `grunt` every time we make a change. This is why there exists `grunt-contrib-watch`. It is a module that looks out for file changes and runs our tasks. Here is the updated `Gruntfile.js`:

```javascript
module.exports = function(grunt) {
    grunt.initConfig({
        concat: {
            javascript: {
                src: 'src/**/*.js',
                dest: 'build/scripts.js'
            }
        },
        uglify: {
            javascript: {
                files: {
                    'build/scripts.min.js': '<%= concat.javascript.dest %>'
                }
            }
        },
        watch: {
            javascript: {
                files: ['<%= concat.javascript.src %>'],
                tasks: ['concat', 'uglify']
            }
        }
    });
    grunt.loadNpmTasks('grunt-contrib-concat');
    grunt.loadNpmTasks('grunt-contrib-uglify');
    grunt.loadNpmTasks('grunt-contrib-watch');
    grunt.registerTask('default', ['concat', 'uglify', 'watch']);
}
```

To get the script working, we have to additionally run `npm install grunt-contrib-watch grunt-contrib-uglify –save`. The command will install the modules and will update the `package.json` file.

The following screenshot shows what the result in the terminal looks like when we call the grunt command:

```
$ grunt
Running "concat:javascript" (concat) task
File build/scripts.js created.

Running "uglify:javascript" (uglify) task
>> 1 file created.

Running "watch" task
Waiting...
>> File "src\a\script.js" changed.
Running "concat:javascript" (concat) task
File build/scripts.js created.

Running "uglify:javascript" (uglify) task
>> 1 file created.

Done, without errors.
Completed in 0.788s at Sun Oct 12 2014 23:36:59 GMT+0300 (FLE Daylight Time) - W
aiting...
```

We can now see how our tasks run and the watching task starts. Once we save changes to a watched file, both the operations — concatenation and minification — are fired again.

Discovering Gulp

Gulp is a build system that automates common tasks. As in Grunt, we can compose our asset pipeline. However, there are a few differences between the two:

- We still have a configuration file, but it is called gulpfile.js.
- Gulp is a streaming-based tool. It doesn't store anything on the disc when it is working. Grunt needs to create temporary files in order to pass data from one task to another, but Gulp keeps the data in the memory.
- Gulp follows the **code-over-configuration** principle. In the gulpfile.js file, we write our tasks like a regular Node.js script. We will see a demonstration of this in a minute.

To use Gulp, we have to install it first. The following command will set up the tool globally:

```
npm install -g gulp
```

We are going to use a few plugins—`gulp-concat`, `gulp-uglify`, and `gulp-rename`. After adding them to our `package.json` file, run `npm install` so that we can install them.

The next step is to create a new `gulpfile.js` file in the root directory of our project and run the `gulp` command. Let's keep the same tasks from the previous section and translate them to Gulp:

```
var gulp = require('gulp');
var concat = require('gulp-concat');
var uglify = require('gulp-uglify');
var rename = require('gulp-rename');

gulp.task('js', function() {
    gulp.src('./src/**/*.js')
    .pipe(concat('scripts.js'))
    .pipe(gulp.dest('./build/'))
    .pipe(rename({suffix: '.min'}))
    .pipe(uglify())
    .pipe(gulp.dest('./build/'))
});
gulp.task('watchers', function() {
    gulp.watch('src/**/*.js', ['js']);
});
gulp.task('default', ['js', 'watchers']);
```

There are a few `require` calls at the top of the file. We initialized the public API of Gulp (the `gulp` object) and the plugins needed for the operations that we want to perform. We need to add all these modules to our `package.json` file. Just after that, we define three tasks by using the (`task_name`, `callback_function`) syntax:

- `js`: This is the task that gets our JavaScript files, pipes them to the plugin that concatenates files, and saves the result. We continue by sending the data to the `uglify` module that minifies our code and in the end, we save a new file with a `.min` suffix.

- `watchers`: With this task, we can monitor our JavaScript for changes and run the `js` task.

- `default`: By default, Gulp runs that part of our file. We may specify the task by adding one more argument to the `gulp` call in the terminal.

The result of the preceding script should look like the following screenshot. Again, we can see how automation happens. The watching part is present, too.

```
$ gulp
[gulp] Using gulpfile code\gulp\gulpfile.js
[gulp] Starting 'js'...
[gulp] Finished 'js' after 11 ms
[gulp] Starting 'watchers'...
[gulp] Finished 'watchers' after 8.88 ms
[gulp] Starting 'default'...
[gulp] Finished 'default' after 7.82 µs
[gulp] Starting 'js'...
[gulp] Finished 'js' after 8.09 ms
```

Test-driven development

Test-driven development is a software development process in which automated tests drive the development cycle of a new product or functionality. It speeds up the development in the long run and tends to produce better code. Nowadays, many frameworks have tools that help you create automated tests. So as developers, we need to write and run tests first before writing any new code. We always check what the result of our work is. In web development, we usually open the browser and interact with our application to see how our code behaves. So, a major part of our time goes into testing. The good news is that we may optimize this process. It is possible to write code that does the job instead of us. Sometimes, relying on manual testing is not the best option, because it takes time. Here are a few benefits of having tests:

- The tests improve the stability of our application
- Automated testing saves time that can be spent in improving or refactoring the system's code
- Test-driven development tends to produce better code over time because it makes us think about better structuring and modular approaches
- Continuous testing helps us develop new features on an existing app since the automated tests will fail if we introduce a code that breaks an old feature
- The tests could be used as documentation, especially for developers who have just joined the team

At the beginning of the process, we want our test to fail. After that, we implement step-by-step the required logic till the test passes. The following diagram shows the process:

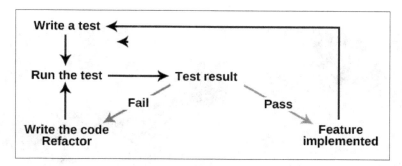

Very often, developers use tools that help them write tests. We are going to use a testing framework called **Mocha**. It is available for Node.js and the browser, and it is one of the most popular solutions when it comes to automated testing. Let's install Mocha and see how TDD works. We will run the following command:

```
npm install mocha -g
```

As we already did several times in the book, we will have the package globally installed. For the purpose of this example, we will assume that our application needs a module that reads external JSON files. Let's create an empty folder and put the following content into a test.js file:

```javascript
var assert = require('assert');
describe('Testing JSON reader', function() {
    it('should get json', function(done) {
        var reader = require('./JSONReader');
        assert.equal(typeof reader, 'object');
        assert.equal(typeof reader.read, 'function');
        done();
    });
});
```

The describe and it functions are Mocha-specific functions. They are global and we have them readily available. The assert module is a native Node.js module that we may use to perform checks. Some of the popular testing frameworks have their own assertion methods. Mocha does not have one, but it works well with libraries such as Chai or Expect.js.

We use `describe` to form a series of tests and `it` to define logical blocks. We assume that there is a `JSONReader.js` file in the current directory and when the module inside is required, we have a public `read` method available. Now, let's run our test with `mocha .\test.js`. The result is as follows:

```
$ mocha .\test.js


 Testing JSON reader
   1) should get json


 0 passing (17ms)
 1 failing

 1) Testing JSON reader should get json:
    Error: Cannot find module 'JSONReader'
     at Function.Module._resolveFilename (module.js:331:15)
     at Function.Module._load (module.js:273:25)
     at Module.require (module.js:357:17)
     at require (module.js:373:17)
```

Of course, our test fails because there is no such file. If we create the file and place the following code in it, our test will pass:

```
// JSONReader.js
module.exports = {
    read: function() {
        // get JSON
        return {};
    }
}
```

The `JSONReader` module exports an object with the help of the `read` public method. We will run `mocha .\test.js` again. However, this time, all the requirements listed in the test are covered. Now, the terminal should look like this:

```
$ mocha .\test.js


 Testing JSON reader
   √ should get json


 1 passing (11ms)
```

Let's assume that our `JSONReader` module has been becoming bigger and bigger. New methods have come in, and different developers have worked on the same file. Our test will still check if the module exists and if there is a `read` function. This is important because somewhere at the beginning of the project, the programmer has used the `JSONReader` module and expects it to have the `read` function available.

In our test, we added just a few assertions. However, in the real world, there will be many more `describe` and `it` blocks. The more cases the test covers, the better. Very often, companies rely on their test suites before releasing a new product version. If there is a test that has failed, they just don't publish anything. In the next few chapters of the book, we will often write tests.

The Model-View-Controller pattern

It's always difficult to start a new project or the implementation of a new feature. We just don't know how to structure our code, what modules to write, and how they are going to communicate. In such cases, we often trust well-known practices — design patterns. Design patterns are reusable solutions to commonly occurring problems. For example, the **Model-View-Controller** pattern has proven to be one of the most effective patterns for web development due to its clear separation of the data, logic, and presentation layers. We will base our social network on a variation of this pattern. The traditional parts and their responsibilities are as follows:

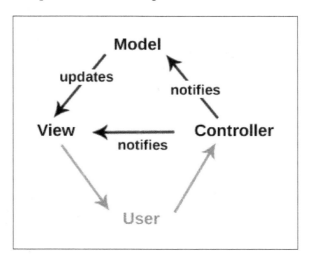

- **Model**: The **Model** is the part that stores the data or the state. It triggers an update on the **View** once there is a change.

- **View**: The **View** is usually the part that the user can see. It is a direct representation of the data or the state of the **Model**.

- **Controller**: The user interacts with the help of the **Controller** (sometimes through the **View**). It can send commands to the **Model** to update its state. In some cases, it can also notify the **View** so that the user can see another representation of the **Model**.

However, in web development (especially the code that runs in the browser), the **View** and the **Controller** share the same functions. Very often, there is no strict distinction between the two. In this book, the controllers will also deal with UI elements. Let's start with the Node.js environment. To simplify the example, we will place our code in a file called server.js. Our application will do only one thing — it will update the value of a variable stored in the memory.

In our context, the **View** will produce HTML markup. Later, that markup will be sent to the browser, as follows:

```
var view = {
    render: function() {
        var html = '';
        html += '<!DOCTYPE html>';
        html += '<html>';
        html += '<head><title>Node.js byexample</title></head>';
        html += '<body>';
        html += '<h1>Status ' + (model.status ? 'on' : 'off') + '</h1>';
        html += '<a href="/on">switch on</a><br />';
        html += '<a href="/off">switch off</a>';
        html += '</body>';
        html += '</html>';
        res.writeHead(200, {'Content-Type': 'text/html'});
        res.end(html + '\n');
    }
};
```

In this code, there is a JavaScript object literal with only one render method. To construct proper content for the h1 tag, we will use the model and its status variable. There are two links as well. The first one changes model.status to true and the second one changes it to false.

The `Model` object is fairly small. Like the **View**, it has only one method:

```
var model = {
    status: false,
    update: function(s) {
        this.status = s;
        view.render();
    }
};
```

Note that **Model** triggers the rendering of the view. It is important to mention here that the Model should not know about the representation of its data in the view layer. All it has to do is send a signal to the view to notify that it is updated.

The last part of our pattern is the **Controller**. We may consider it as an entry point of our script. If we are building a Node.js server, this is the function that accepts the `request` and `response` object:

```
var http = require('http'), res;
var controller = function(request, response) {
    res = response;
    if(request.url === '/on') {
        model.update(true);
    } else if(request.url === '/off') {
        model.update(false);
    } else {
        view.render();
    }
}
http.createServer(controller).listen(1337, '127.0.0.1');
console.log('Server running at http://127.0.0.1:1337/');
```

We cached the `response` parameter in a global variable so we that can access it from other functions.

This is similar to the instance that occurred at the beginning of this chapter where we used the `request.url` property to control the flow of the application. The preceding code changes the state of the model when the user visits the /on or /off URLs. If it does not, then it simply triggers the `render` function of the view.

The Model-View-Controller pattern fits Node.js well. As we saw, it can be easily implemented. Since it is really popular, there are modules and even frameworks that use this concept. In the next few chapters, we will see how the pattern works in large-scale applications.

Introducing the REST API concept

REST stands for **Representational State Transfer**. By definition, it is an architectural principle of the Web. In practice, it is a set of rules that simplify client-server communication. A lot of companies provide REST APIs because they are simple and highly scalable.

To better understand what REST exactly means, let's take a simple example. We have an online store and we want to manage the users in our system. We have the backend logic implemented in various controllers. We want to trigger functionalities there via HTTP requests. In other words, we need an application program interface for these controllers. We start by planning the URLs to access our server. If we follow the REST architecture, then we may have the following routes:

- GET requests to /users return a list of all the users in the system

- POST requests to /users create new user

- PUT requests to /users/24 edit the data of a user with the unique identification number 24

- DELETE requests to /users/24 delete the profile of a user with the unique identification number 24

There is a resource defined — **user**. The URL is what makes REST simple. The GET request is used to retrieve data, POST is for storing, PUT is for editing and DELETE is for removing records.

Some parts of our small social network will be based on the REST architecture. We will have controllers that handle the four types of requests and perform the necessary operations. However, before we reach that part of the book, let's write a simple Node.js server that accepts GET, POST, PUT, and DELETE requests. The following code goes to a file called server.js:

```
var http = require('http');
var url = require('url');
var controller = function(req, res) {
    var message = '';
    switch(req.method) {
```

```
        case 'GET': message = "Thats GET message"; break;
        case 'POST': message = "That's POST message"; break;
        case 'PUT': message = "That's PUT message"; break;
        case 'DELETE': message = "That's DELETE message"; break;
    }
    res.writeHead(200, {'Content-Type': 'text/html'});
    res.end(message + '\n');
}
http.createServer(controller).listen(1337, '127.0.0.1');
console.log('Server running at http://127.0.0.1:1337/');
```

The `req` object has a `method` property. It tells us about the type of the request. We may run the preceding server with `node .\server.js` and send different types of requests. In order to test it, we will use the popular `curl` command:

```
$ curl http://localhost:1337/
That's GET message
```

Let's try a more complex PUT request. The following example uses cURL. It is a command-line tool that helps you run requests. In our case, we will perform a PUT request to our server:

```
$ curl -X PUT -d book="Node.js by example" http://localhost:1337/
That's PUT message
```

We changed the request method with the `-X` option. Along with this, we passed a variable called `book` with the `Node.js by example` value. However, our server does not have code that processes parameters. We will add the following function to our `server.js`:

```
var qs = require('querystring');
var processRequest = function(req, callback) {
    var body = '';
    req.on('data', function (data) {
        body += data;
    });
    req.on('end', function () {
        callback(qs.parse(body));
    });
}
```

The code accepts the `req` object and a callback function because collecting the data is an asynchronous operation. The `body` variable is filled with the incoming data and once all the chunks are collected, we trigger the callback by passing the parsed body of the request. Here is the updated controller:

```
var controller = function(req, res) {
    var message = '';
    switch(req.method) {
        case 'GET': message = "That's GET message"; break;
        case 'POST': message = "That's POST message"; break;
        case 'PUT':
            processRequest(req, function(data) {
                message = "That's PUT message. You are editing " +
                    data.book + " book.";
                res.writeHead(200, {'Content-Type': 'text/html'});
                res.end(message + "\n");
            });
            return;
        break;
        case 'DELETE': message = "That's DELETE message"; break;
    }
    res.writeHead(200, {'Content-Type': 'text/html'});
    res.end(message + '\n');
}
```

Note that we called `return` in the PUT catch statement. We did this so that the application flow stops there and waits till the request is processed. This is the result in the terminal:

```
$ curl -X PUT -d book="Node.js by example" http://localhost:1337/
That's PUT message. You are reading "Node.js by example" book.
```

Summary

The developing of software is a complex task. Like every complex process, it needs planning. It needs a good base and a well-designed architecture. In this chapter, we saw a few different aspects of planning a big Node.js application. In the next chapter, we will learn how to manage our assets.

3
Managing Assets

The first two chapters were a good introduction to the building blocks and structures of Node.js application development. We learned about the fundamentals of the technology and revealed important patterns such as Model-View-Controller. We talked about test-driven development and REST APIs. In this chapter, we will create the base of our social network. The proper delivery and management of an application's assets is an essential part of the system. In most of the cases, it determines our workflow. We will go through the following topics in this chapter:

- Serving files with Node.js
- CSS preprocessing
- Packing client-side JavaScript
- Delivering HTML templates

Serving files with Node.js

Node.js differs from the usual Linux-Apache-MySQL-PHP setup. We have to write the server that handles the incoming request. When the user requires an image from our backend, Node.js doesn't serve it automatically. The very first file of our social network will be server.js with the following content:

```
var http = require('http');
var fs = require('fs');
   var path = require('path');

var files = {};
var port = 9000;
var host = '127.0.0.1';
```

```
var assets = function(req, res) {
  // ...
};

var app = http.createServer(assets).listen(port, host);
console.log("Listening on " + host + ":" + port);
```

We require three native modules that we will use to drive the server and deliver assets. The last two lines of the preceding code run the server and print a message to the console.

For now, the entry point of our application is the `assets` function. The main purpose of this method is to read files from the hard disk and serve it to the users. We will use `req.url` to fetch the current request path. When a web browser accesses our server and requests `http://localhost:9000/static/css/styles.css` in the browser, `req.url` will be equal to `/static/css/styles.css`. From this point onwards, we have a few tasks to handle:

- Checking whether the file exists and if not, sending a proper message (HTTP error code) to the user
- Reading the file and finding out its extension
- Sending the file's content to the browser with the correct content type

The last point is an important one. Serving files with a wrong or missing content type may cause problems. The browser may not be able to recognize and process the resource properly.

To make the process smooth, we will create a separate function for each of the tasks mentioned. The shortest one is the one that sends an error message to the user:

```
var sendError = function(message, code) {
  if(code === undefined) {
    code = 404;
  }
  res.writeHead(code, {'Content-Type': 'text/html'});
  res.end(message);
}
```

By default, the value of the `code` variable is `404`, which means **Not Found**. However, there are different types of errors, such as client errors (4XX) and server errors (5XX). It is good to leave an option to change the error's code.

Let's say that we have the content of the file and its extension. We need a function that recognizes the correct content type and delivers the resource to the client. For the sake of simplicity, we will perform a simple string-to-string check of the file's extension. The following code does exactly that:

```
var serve = function(file) {
  var contentType;
  switch(file.ext.toLowerCase()) {
    case "css": contentType = "text/css"; break;
    case "html": contentType = "text/html"; break;
    case "js": contentType = "application/javascript"; break;
    case "ico": contentType = "image/ico"; break;
    case "json": contentType = "application/json"; break;
    case "jpg": contentType = "image/jpeg"; break;
    case "jpeg": contentType = "image/jpeg"; break;
    case "png": contentType = "image/png"; break;
    default: contentType = "text/plain";
  }
  res.writeHead(200, {'Content-Type': contentType});
  res.end(file.content);
}
```

The `serve` method accepts a `file` object with two properties—`ext` and `content`. In the next few chapters, we will probably add more file types to the list. However, for now, serving JavaScript, CSS, HTML, JPG, and PNG images is enough.

The last task that we have to cover is the actual reading of the file. Node.js has a built-in module to read files called `fs`. We will use the asynchronous versions of its methods. With synchronous functions, the JavaScript engine may be blocked till the particular operation is fully executed. In this case, that is a reading of a file. In asynchronous programming, we allow our program to execute the rest of the code. In this scenario, we normally pass a callback—a function that will be executed when the operation ends:

```
var readFile = function(filePath) {
  if(files[filePath]) {
      serve(files[filePath]);
    } else {
      fs.readFile(filePath, function(err, data) {
        if(err) {
          sendError('Error reading ' + filePath + '.');
```

```
            return;
        }
        files[filePath] = {
            ext: filePath.split(".").pop(),
            content: data
        };
        serve(files[filePath]);
    });
  }
}
```

The function accepts the path and opens the file. If the file is missing or there is a problem reading it, it sends an error to the user. In the beginning, we defined a `files` variable, which is an empty object. Every time we read a file, we are storing its content there so that the next time we read it, we don't have to access the disk again. Every I/O operation, such as reading a file, takes time. By using this simple caching logic, we improve the performance of our application. If everything is okay, we call the `serve` method.

Here is how you combine all the preceding snippets:

```
var http = require('http');
var fs = require('fs');
var path = require('path');
var files = {};
var port = 9000;

var assets = function(req, res) {
  var sendError = function(message, code) { ... }
  var serve = function(file) { ... }
  var readFile = function(filePath) { ... }

  readFile(path.normalize(__dirname + req.url));
}

var app = http.createServer(assets).listen(port, '127.0.0.1');
console.log("Listening on 127.0.0.1:" + port);
```

Every HTTP request sent to our server is processed by the `assets` handler. We compose the file's path, starting from the current directory. The `path.normalize` parameter guarantees that our string looks alright on different operating systems. For example, it does not contain multiple slashes.

CSS preprocessing

CSS preprocessors are tools that accept source and produce CSS. Very often, the input is similar to the CSS language with regard to the syntax. However, the main idea of preprocessing is to add features that are missing and, at the same time, wanted by the community. Over the past few years, CSS preprocessing has become a hot topic. It comes with lots of benefits and the concept has been warmly accepted by the community. There are two main CSS preprocesors—**Less** (`http://lesscss.org/`) and **Sass** (`http://sass-lang.com/`). Sass is based on the Ruby language and it requires more effort to run it in a Node.js project. So in this book, we are going to use Less.

In the previous chapter, we talked about building systems and task runners. CSS preprocessing and a few other tasks that we will talk about in a bit should happen automatically. Gulp seems like a good option. Let's move forward and add a `package.json` file where we will describe all the Gulp-related modules that we need:

```
{
    "name": "nodejs-by-example",
    "version": "0.0.1",
    "description": "Node.js by example",
    "scripts": {
        "start": "node server.js"
    },
    "dependencies": {
        "gulp": "3.8.8",
        "gulp-less": "1.3.6",
        "gulp-rename": "~1.2.0",
        "gulp-minify-css": "~0.3.11"
    }
}
```

The setting of `"start": "node server.js"` will allow us to type `npm start` and run our server. The dependencies that we will start with are as follows:

- Gulp itself
- `gulp-less`: This is a plugin that wraps the Less preprocessor
- `gulp-rename`: This changes the name of the produced file
- `gulp-minify-css`: This compresses our CSS

So, along with `server.js`, we now have `package.json`. We run `npm install` and the package manager adds a `node_modules` directory containing the modules. Let's define our Gulp tasks in another file named `gulpfile.js`:

```
var path = require('path');
var gulp = require('gulp');
var less = require('gulp-less');
var rename = require("gulp-rename");
var minifyCSS = require('gulp-minify-css');

gulp.task('css', function() {
  gulp.src('./less/styles.less')
  .pipe(less({
    paths: [ path.join(__dirname, 'less', 'includes') ]
  }))
  .pipe(gulp.dest('./static/css'))
  .pipe(minifyCSS({keepBreaks:true}))
  .pipe(rename({suffix: '.min'}))
  .pipe(gulp.dest('./static/css'));
});

gulp.task('watchers', function() {
  gulp.watch('less/**/*.less', ['css']);
});

gulp.task('default', ['css', 'watchers']);
```

We start with two tasks — css and `watchers`. The first one expects us to have a `less` directory and a `styles.less` file inside. This will be our entry point to all the CSS styles. As seen from the Gulp task, we pipe the content of the file to the preprocessor and export the result to the `static/css` directory. Since everything with Gulp is a stream, we can continue and minify the CSS, rename the file to `styles.min.css`, and export it to the same folder.

We do not want to run the building processes by ourselves every time we make changes to a file. So, we register `watchers` for the files in the `less` folder. A watcher is a process that monitors specific files and notifies the rest of the system once these files are changed.

At the end of this step, our project looks like this:

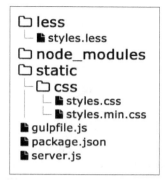

Packing client-side JavaScript

As with CSS, our goal should be to serve only one JavaScript file to the client's browser. We do not want to force the user to make more than one request, because this is less efficient and it means that the web browser takes longer to process and display the content of the page. Nowadays, the client-side part of applications is fairly complex. As with complex systems, we split our logic into different modules. Often, different modules mean different files. Thankfully, Node.js is full of tools that can be used to pack JavaScript. Let's see two of the most popular tools.

Concatenating with Gulp

Gulp, as a build system, has several modules to concatenate files. The one that we are interested in is called `gulp-concat`. Let's add it to the `package.json` file:

```
"dependencies": {
  "gulp": "3.8.8",
  "gulp-less": "1.3.6",
  "gulp-rename": "1.2.0",
  "gulp-minify-css": "0.3.11",
  "gulp-concat": "2.4.1"
}
```

The next step is to write a task that uses it. Again, we will use the `src` and `dest` Gulp methods, and in between is the concatenation:

```
var concat = require('gulp-concat');

gulp.task('js', function() {
  gulp.src('./js/*.js')
  .pipe(concat('scripts.js'))
  .pipe(gulp.dest('./static/js'))
});
```

It's important to mention that the files will be added to the final file in alphabetical order. So, we should be careful whenever there are some code dependencies. If this is the case, we should name the files in such a way that their names start with a unique number—01, 02, 03, and so on.

The next logical task that we will do is to minify our JavaScript. Like the Less compilation, we want to serve a file that is as small as possible. The module that will help us achieve this is `gulp-uglify`. Again, we should add it to the `package.json` file (`"gulp-uglify": "1.0.1"`). After this, a little tweak to our newly created task will minify the JavaScript:

```
var concat = require('gulp-concat');
var uglify = require('gulp-uglify');

gulp.task('js', function() {
  gulp.src('./js/*.js')
  .pipe(concat('scripts.js'))
  .pipe(gulp.dest('./static/js'))
  .pipe(uglify())
  .pipe(rename({suffix: '.min'}))
  .pipe(gulp.dest('./static/js'))
});
```

Note that we used the `gulp-rename` plugin again. This is necessary because we want to produce a different file.

Modularity in the browser with RequireJS

While building software, one of the most important concepts to think about is the splitting of our system into modules. Node.js has a nice built-in system to write modules. We mentioned this in *Chapter 1, Node.js Fundamentals*. We encapsulate our code in a single file and use `module.exports` or `exports` to create the public API. Later, via the `require` function, we access the created functionalities.

However, for the client-side JavaScript, we do not have such a built-in system. We need to use an additional library that allows us to define modules. There are several possible solutions. The first one that we will take a look at is RequireJS (http://requirejs.org/). We will download the library (version 2.1.16) from the official site and include it in our page like this:

```
<script data-main="scripts/main" src="scripts/require.js">
</script>
```

The key attribute here is data-main. It tells RequireJS about our application's entry point. In fact, we should have the scripts/main.js file in our project's folder to get the preceding line working. In main.js, we can use the require global function:

```
// scripts/main.js
require(["modules/ajax", "modules/router"], function(ajax, router) {
    // ... our logic
});
```

Let's say that our code in main.js depends on two other modules—the Ajax wrapper and router. We describe these dependencies in an array and provide a callback, which is later executed with two parameters. These parameters are actually references to the necessary modules.

The defining of modules is possible with the help of another global function—define. Here is how the Ajax wrapper looks:

```
// modules/ajax.js
define(function () {
    // the Ajax request implementation
    ...
    // public API
    return {
        request: function() { ... }
    }
});
```

By default, behind the scenes, RequireJS resolves the dependencies asynchronously. In other words, it performs an HTTP request for every required module. In some cases, this may lead to performance issues because every request takes time. Thankfully, RequireJS has a tool (optimizer) that solves the problem. It can bundle all the modules into a single file. The tool is available for Node.js too and it is distributed with the requirejs package:

```
npm install -g requirejs
```

After a successful installation, we will have the `r.js` command in our terminal. The basic call looks like this:

```
// in code_requirejs folder
r.js -o build.js
```

As with Grunt and Gulp, we have a file that instructs RequireJS on how to work. The following is a snippet that covers our example:

```
// build.js
({
    baseUrl: ".",
    paths: {},
    name: "main",
    out: "main-built.js"
})
```

The `name` property is the entry point and `out` is the resulting file. It's nice that we have the `paths` property available. It is a place where we can describe the modules directly; for example, `jquery: "some/other/jquery"`. Later in our code, we do not have to write the full path to the files. Just a simple `require(['jquery'], ...)` is enough.

By default, the output of the `r.js` command is minified. If we add an `optimize=none` argument to the command in the terminal, we will get the following:

```
// main-built.js
define('modules/ajax',[],function () {
    ...
});

define('modules/router',[],function () {
    ...
});

require(['modules/ajax', 'modules/router'], function(ajax, router) {
    ...
});
define("main", function(){});
```

The `main-built.js` file contains the main module and its dependencies.

Moving from Node.js to the browser with Browserify

RequireJS indeed solves the problem with modularity. However, it makes us write more code. Also, we should always describe our dependencies by following a strict format. Let's look at the code that we used in the previous section:

```
require(['modules/ajax', 'modules/router'], function(ajax, router) {
    ...
});
```

It is indeed better if we use the following code:

```
var ajax = require('modules/ajax');
var router = require('modules/router');
```

The code is much simpler now. This is how we should fetch a module in the Node.js environment. It would be nice if we could use the same approach in the browser.

Browserify (http://browserify.org/) is a module that brings the require module of Node.js to the browser. Let's install it first by using the following code:

npm install -g browserify

Similarly, to illustrate how the tool works, we will create the main.js, ajax.js and router.js files. This time, we are not going to use a global function such as define. Instead, we will use the usual Node.js module.exports:

```
// main.js
var ajax = require('./modules/ajax');
var router = require('./modules/router');

// modules/ajax.js
module.exports = function() {};

// modules/router.js
module.exports = function() {};
```

By default, Browserify comes as a command-line tool. We need to provide an entry point and an output file:

```
browserify ./main.js -o main-built.js
```

The result in the compiled file is as follows:

```
// main-built.js
(function e(t,n,r){function s(o,u){if(!n[o]){if(!t[o]){var
a=typeof require=="function"&&require;if(!u&&a)return
a(o,!0);if(i)return i(o,!0);var f=new Error("Cannot find module
'"+o+"'");throw f.code="MODULE_NOT_FOUND",f}var
l=n[o]={exports:{}};t[o][0].call(l.exports,function(e){var
n=t[o][1][e];return s(n?n:e)},l,l.exports,e,t,n,r)}return
n[o].exports}var i=typeof require=="function"&&require;for(var
o=0;o<r.length;o++)s(r[o]);return
s})({1:[function(require,module,exports){
var ajax = require('./modules/ajax');
var router = require('./modules/router');
},{"./modules/ajax":2,"./modules/router":3}],2:[function(require,
module,exports){
module.exports = function() {};
},{}],3:[function(require,module,exports){
module.exports=require(2)
},{".../modules/ajax.js":2}]},{},[1]);
```

Note that along with the modules, the compiled file also contains the require function's definition and implementation. It's really just a few bytes of code that makes Browserify one of the most popular ways to deliver modular JavaScript in the browser. This is what we are going to use in the next few chapters.

We have started a Gulp setup. Let's add Browserify there. We have already made a concatenation of the JavaScript. Let's replace it with Browserify. We will add the module to the `package.json` file as follows:

```
"dependencies": {
  "gulp": "3.8.8",
  "gulp-less": "1.3.6",
  "gulp-rename": "1.2.0",
  "gulp-minify-css": "0.3.11",
  "gulp-concat": "2.4.1",
  "gulp-uglify": "1.0.1",
  "gulp-browserify": "0.5.0"
}
```

After running `npm install`, we will get the plugin installed and ready to use. We need to make two changes, replacing `concat` with `browserify` and pointing out the application's main file:

```
var browserify = require('gulp-browserify');
var uglify = require('gulp-uglify');

gulp.task('js', function() {
  gulp.src('./js/app.js')
  .pipe(browserify())
  .pipe(gulp.dest('./static/js'))
  .pipe(uglify())
  .pipe(rename({suffix: '.min'}))
  .pipe(gulp.dest('./static/js'))
});
```

Now, the `src` method accepts only one file. It's our entry point. This is the place where Browserify starts resolving dependencies. The rest is the same. We still use `uglify` for minification and `rename` to change the file's name.

Delivering HTML templates

In the previous sections, you saw how you can package CSS and JavaScript for the browser. At the end of this chapter, we will explore the various ways to deliver HTML. In the context of client-side applications, the templates still contain HTML. However, we need a dynamic way to render and fill them with data.

Defining the templates in script tags

The Ember.js framework adopts the concept of adding HTML templates directly into the page by using the popular **handlebars** (http://handlebarsjs.com/) template engine. However, since we do not want to mess up the markup that is already there, we place them in the `<script>` tags. The good thing about this is that if we set a custom value of the `type` attribute, the browser does not process the code inside. Here's a demonstration of this:

```
<script type="text/x-handlebars" id="my-template">
    <p>Hello, <strong> </strong>!</p>
</script>
```

Since the tag has an `id` attribute, we can get its content easily in the following way:

```
var template = document.querySelector('#my-template').innerHTML;
```

The benefit of this technique is that the template is on the page and we have instant access to it. Also, templates only display the desired content after being processed by JavaScript. So, if JavaScript is not enabled in the browser, we do not want to display the unprocessed raw template. A major problem with this concept is the fact that we will flood our HTML page with a lot of code. If we have a big application, then the user will have to download all the templates even if he/she uses only a part of it.

Loading the template externally

It's also a common practice to define the templates as external files and load them on the page with an Ajax request. The following pseudocode uses jQuery's `get` method to do the job:

```
$.get('/templates/template.html', function(html) {
    // ...
});
```

We have clear markup, but the user has to make an additional HTTP request in order to fetch the template. This approach makes the code more complex because the process is asynchronous. It also makes the processing and rendering of the content slower than the preceding method.

Writing HTML inside the JavaScript

With the rise of mobile applications, many big companies have started developing their own frameworks. Since these companies have enough resources, they usually produce something interesting. For example, Facebook created a framework called **React** (`http://facebook.github.io/react/`). It defines its templates directly in the JavaScript as follows:

```
<script type="text/jsx">
  var HelloMessage = React.createClass({
    render: function() {
      // Note: the following line is invalid JavaScript,
        // and only works using React parser.
      return <div>Hello {this.props.name}</div>;
    }
  });
</script>
```

The developers from Facebook adopted the first technique mentioned in this section. They put some code inside a `<script>` tag. In order to get things working, they have their own parser. It processes the script and converts it into valid JavaScript.

There are solutions that do not have templates in the form of HTML. There are tools that use templates written in JSON or YAML. For example, **AbsurdJS** (`http://absurdjs.com/`) can keep its template inside the JavaScript class definition as follows:

```
body: {
  'section.content#home': {
    nav: [
      { 'a[href="#" class="link"]': 'A' },
      { 'a[href="#" class="link"]': 'B' },
      { 'a[href="#" class="link"]': 'C' }
    ]
  },
  footer: {
    p: 'Text in the Footer'
  }
}
```

Precompiling templates

Another popular way to deliver templates to the client side is by using precompilation. This is what we are going to use in our project. Precompilation is a process that converts the HTML template to a JavaScript object, which is ready for use in our code. This approach has several benefits, some of which are as follows:

- We do not have to think about accessing the HTML template
- The markup is still separated from the JavaScript code
- We do not lose time in fetching and processing the HTML

Different client-side frameworks have different tools to precompile templates. We will cover this in detail later, but the instrument that we are going to use for our social network application is called Ractive.js (`http://www.ractivejs.org/`). It's a client-side framework that was originally developed by the people at TheGuardian to produce a news application. It's cross-browser and it performs well on mobile devices.

In order to transform our HTML into Ractive-precompiled templates, we need two new modules in the `package.json` file:

```
"ractive": "0.6.1",
"gulp-tap": "0.1.3"
```

The `gulp-tap` plugin allows us to process every file sent to the Gulp's pipeline. Here is the new task that we have to add to the `gulpfile.js` file:

```
var Ractive = require('ractive');
var tap = require('gulp-tap');

gulp.task('templates', function() {
  gulp.src('./tpl/**/*.html')
  .pipe(tap(function(file, t) {
    var precompiled = Ractive.parse(file.contents.toString());
    precompiled = JSON.stringify(precompiled);
    file.contents = new Buffer('module.exports = ' + precompiled);
  }))
  .pipe(rename(function(path) {
    path.extname = '.js';
  }))
  .pipe(gulp.dest('./tpl'))
});

gulp.task('default', ['css', 'templates', 'js', 'watchers']);
```

`Ractive.parse` returns the precompiled template. Since it is a JavaScript object, we use `JSON.stringify` to convert it to a string. We use Browserify to control our client-side modularity so `module.exports` is attached in front of the template's code. In the end, we use `gulp-rename` and produce a JavaScript file.

Let's say that we have a `/tpl/template.html` file with the following content:

```
<section>
  <h1>Hello {{name}}</h1>
</section>
```

When we run the `gulp` command, we will receive `/tpl/template.js`, which contains the JavaScript that is equivalent to the preceding markup:

```
module.exports =
{"v":1,"t":[{"t":7,"e":"section","f":[{"t":7,"e":"h1","f":["Hello ",{"t":2,"r":"name"}]}]}]}
```

It probably looks strange now, but in the next few chapters, you will see how you can use such templates.

Summary

Assets are a major part of web applications. Often, companies do not pay enough attention to this part, which leads to slower loading time and increased web hosting costs, especially when your site grows in popularity. In this chapter, we saw that it is important to find the right setup and deliver the images, CSS, JavaScript, and HTML in the most efficient way.

In the next chapter, we will start working heavily on our social network. We will explore the world of the Model-View-Controller pattern.

4
Developing the Model-View-Controller Layers

In the previous chapter, we learned how to prepare the assets needed by our application. It is time to move forward and start writing the base levels of our social network. In this chapter, we will use the Model-View-Controller pattern and prepare our code base to implement the future of our application. Here is what we will talk about in this chapter:

- Transforming the code from the previous chapter to a better file structure
- Implementing a router that works in both backend and frontend environments
- Briefly introducing Ractive.js — a framework that we will use in the client-side part of the project
- Developing the main file of the application
- Implementing controller, view, and model classes

Evolving the current setup

Writing software is difficult. Often, it's a process of change. In order to evolve and extend our systems, we have to make changes in the code. We will take the code from the previous chapter and introduce a couple of new folders and files. We will change the architecture a bit so that it fits in the development afterwards.

Directory structure

It is a common practice to split the logic into frontend and backend. We are going to follow the same approach. Here is the new file structure:

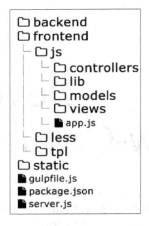

The `backend` directory will contain files used in the Node.js environment. As we can see, we moved the files that were previously in the main directory to the `frontend` folder. These are the files that produce the resources placed in the `static` directory. We still have the necessary `gulpfile.js`, `package.json`, and `server.js` files that contain the code of the Node.js server.

Forming the main server handlers

So far, our server only has one request handler—`assets`. Here is how we started our server in the previous chapter:

```
var app = http.createServer(assets).listen(port, '127.0.0.1');
```

Along with the serving assets, we have to add two other handlers, which are as follows:

- **API handler**: The client-side part of our application will communicate with the backend via the REST API. We introduced this concept in *Chapter 2, Architecting the Project.*

- **Page handler**: If the request that comes to the server is not for an asset or API resource, we will serve an HTML page, which is the page that normal users will see.

It's not really a good idea to keep everything in a single file. So, the first step is to extract the `assets` function to its own module:

```
// backend/Assets.js
module.exports = function(req, res) {
...
}

// server.js
var Assets = require('./backend/Assets');
```

We will follow a similar approach and create a `backend/API.js` file. It will be responsible for the REST API. We will use JSON as a format to transfer data. The simplest code that we can use for this is as follows:

```
// backend/API.js
module.exports = function(req, res) {
  res.writeHead(200, {'Content-Type': 'application/json'});
  res.end('{}' + '\n');
}
```

Setting the correct `Content-Type` value is important. If it is missing or if it is a wrong value, then the browser that receives the response may not process the result properly. In the end, we are returning a minimal empty JSON string.

Towards the end, we will add `backend/Default.js`. This is the file that will generate the HTML page that users will see in the browser:

```
// backend/Default.js
var fs = require('fs');
var html = fs.readFileSync(__dirname + '/tpl/page.html').
toString('utf8');
module.exports = function(req, res) {
  res.writeHead(200, {'Content-Type': 'text/html'});
  res.end(html + '\n');
}
```

The content of `Default.js` looks similar to `API.js`. We will again set the `Content-Type` value and use the `end()` method of the `response` object. However, here we load the HTML Unicode string from an external file, which is stored in `backend/tpl/page.html`. The reading of the file is synchronous, and it happens only once in the beginning. Here is the code of `page.html`:

```html
<!doctype html>
<html lang="en">
<head>
  <meta charset="utf-8">
  <title>Node.js by example</title>
  <meta http-equiv="Content-Type" content="text/html;
charset=utf-8" />
  <meta name="description" content="Node.js by examples">
  <meta name="author" content="Packt">
  <link rel="stylesheet" href="/static/css/styles.css">
</head>
<body>
  <script src="/static/js/ractive.js"></script>
  <script src="/static/js/app.js"></script>
</body>
</html>
```

This is a basic HTML5 boilerplate code containing head, body tag, CSS, and JavaScript imports. Our application will only need the following two JavaScript files to work:

- `ractive.js`: This is the framework that we will use in the client-side. More about this will be discussed in the next few sections.

- `app.js`: This is our client-side JavaScript. As seen in a previous chapter, it is produced by the Gulp setup.

Having mentioned the handlers in the backend, we are ready to jump into the code that will be run in the browser.

Implementing the router

Almost every web application needs a router, which is a component that acts as a front door and accepts the incoming queries. It analyzes the parameters of the request and decides which module of our system will serve the result.

We are using JavaScript language in the backend (via Node.js) and frontend (interpreted by the web browser). In this section, we will write a router that works in both the sides of our application. Let's start examining what the Node.js part needs:

```
// frontend/js/lib/Router.js
module.exports = function() {
  return {
    routes: [],
    add: function(path, handler) {
      // ...
    },
    check: function(fragment, params) {
      // ...
    }
  }
};
```

`Router.js` exports two methods. The first one registers routes by accepting a path and a handler function, which will be called if the current URL matches the path. The `check` function simply performs the actual check.

Here is how the `add` method looks:

```
add: function(path, handler) {
  if(typeof path === 'function') {
    handler = path;
    path = '';
  }
  this.routes.push({
    path: path,
    handler: handler
  });
  return this;
}
```

We can skip the `path` parameter and just register a function that matches every route. It is nice to support such behavior in cases where we want to define a default route.

The `check` function is slightly more complex. It not only covers simple string-to-string matching, but should also support dynamic parameters. We are going to use `:id` for these dynamic parameters. For example:

- `/home`: This matches `http://localhost/home`

- `/user/feed`: This matches `http://localhost/user/feed`

- `/user/:id/profile`: This matches `http://localhost/user/45/profile`

- `/user/:id/:action`: This matches `http://localhost/user/45/update`

In order to implement this functionality, we will use regular expressions in the following way:

```
check: function(f, params) {
  var fragment, vars;
  if(typeof f !== 'undefined') {
    fragment = f.replace(/^\//, '');
  } else {
    fragment = this.getFragment();
  }
  for(var i=0; i<this.routes.length; i++) {
    var match, path = this.routes[i].path;
    path = path.replace(/^\//, '');
    vars = path.match(/:[^\s/]+/g);
    var r = new RegExp('^' + path.replace(/:[^\s/]+/g,
      '([\\w-]+)'));
    match = fragment.match(r);
    if(match) {
      match.shift();
      var matchObj = {};
      if(vars) {
        for(var j=0; j<vars.length; j++) {
          var v = vars[j];
          matchObj[v.substr(1, v.length)] = match[j];
        }
      }
      this.routes[i].handler.apply({},
(params || []).concat([matchObj]));
      return this;
    }
  }
  return false;
}
```

Let's go through the function line by line. The arguments of the method are `f` and `parameters`. The fragment is actually a path. This is the URL against which we run the check. In the `add` method, we added a handler that should be fired once we have a match. It would be nice if we were able to send additional variables to this method. The `parameters` argument covers this functionality. We can send an array, which is later translated to the parameters of the handler.

The function continues with the checking whether the fragment is defined. In the Node.js environment, we have to send the URL. However, since we will use the same code in the browser, we define a `getFragment` helper method:

```
getFragment: function() {
  var fragment = '';
  fragment = this.clearSlashes(decodeURI(window.location.pathname
    + location.search));
  fragment = fragment.replace(/\?(.*)$/, '');
  fragment = this.root !== '/' ? fragment.replace(this.root, '') :
    fragment;
  return this.clearSlashes(fragment);
}
```

The main idea of this helper is to get the current URL of the browser by using the global `window.location` object. You may notice another `clearSlashes` function. It does exactly what its name suggests. It removes the unnecessary slashes from the beginning and end of the string:

```
clearSlashes: function(path) {
  return path.toString().replace(/\/$/, '').replace(/^\//, '');
}
```

Let's get back to the `check` function. We will continue looping over the registered routes. For every route, we perform the following actions:

- We prepare a regular expression by extracting the dynamic parts (if any); for example, `users/:id/:action` is transformed to `test/([\w-]+)/([\w-]+)`. We will use this later in the book.

- We check whether the regular expression matches the fragment. If it does, then we compose an array of parameters and call the route's handler.

It's interesting that if we pass our own path (the fragment), we can use the same JavaScript in both the Node.js and browser environments.

The client side of the application will need two other methods. So far, we have routes' registration and checking whether these rules match the URL specifically. This may work for the backend, but in the frontend, we need to constantly monitor the current browser location. That's why we will add the following function:

```
listen: function() {
  var self = this;
  var current = self.getFragment();
  var fn = function() {
    if(current !== self.getFragment()) {
      current = self.getFragment();
      self.check(current);
    }
  }
  clearInterval(this.interval);
  this.interval = setInterval(fn, 50);
  return this;
}
```

By using `setInterval`, we will run the `fn` closure again and again. It checks whether the current URL has changed, and if it has, then it fires the `check` method, which has already been explained.

The last addition to the class is the `navigate` function:

```
navigate: function(path) {
  path = path ? path : '';
  history.pushState(null, null, this.root + this.clearSlashes(path));
  return this;
}
```

We will probably want to change the current page from within our code. The router is a good instrument for this. Once we change the browser's URL, the class automatically calls the right handler. The preceding code uses the HTML5 history API (`http://diveintohtml5.info/history.html`). The `pushState` method changes the string of the browser's address bar.

Adding the `navigate` method, we finalized our router, which is a module that can be used in the backend as it is in the frontend. Before we continue with the Model-View-Controller components, we will briefly introduce Ractive.js — the framework that we will use as a driving power for user interface development.

Introducing Ractive.js

Ractive.js is a framework developed by TheGuardian, a well-known news organization (http://www.theguardian.com/). It simplifies the DOM interaction and provides features like two-way data binding and custom component creation. We are not going to cover all the capabilities of the framework now. A new feature will be introduced in later chapters.

In complex web applications like ours, it is extremely important to split different logical parts into components. Thankfully, Ractive.js provides an interface for this. Here is how a typical component looks:

```
var Component = Ractive.extend({
  template: '<div><h1>{{title}}</h1></div>',
  data: {
    title: 'Hello world'
  }
});
var instance = new Component();
instance.render(document.'body);
```

The `template` property contains an HTML markup or (as in our case) a precompiled template. The data object is accessible inside our templates. Ractive.js uses **mustache** (http://mustache.github.io/) as a template language. We can add another property called `el` and directly choose where the component will be rendered after initialization. However, there is another way — the `render` method. This method accepts a DOM element. In the preceding code, this is just the body of the page.

Similarly, like the DOM tree in the browser, we will need the nesting of the components. This is nicely handled by the framework by introducing a custom tag definition, as demonstrated in the following example:

```
var SubComponent = Ractive.extend({
    template: '<small>Hello there!</small>'
});
var Component = Ractive.extend({
  template: '\
    <div>\
        <h1>{{title}}</h1>\
        <my-subcomponent />\
    </div>\
  ',
```

```
  data: {
    title: 'Hello world'
  },
  components: {
    'my-subcomponent': SubComponent
  }
});
var instance = new Component();
instance.render(document.querySelector('body'));
```

Every component may have a hash map object (`components`) that defines our
custom tags. We can nest as many components as we want. The HTML produced
by the preceding code is as follows:

```
<div>
  <h1>Hello world</h1>
  <small>Hello there!</small>
</div>
```

There are several ways to establish communication between different Ractive.js
components. The most convenient one involves triggering and listening to events.
Let's check the following code snippet:

```
var Component = Ractive.extend({
  template: '<div><h1>{{title}}</h1></div>',
  notifyTheOutsideWorld: function() {
    this.fire('custom-event');
  }
});
var instance = new Component();
instance.on('custom-event', function() {
  this.set('title', 'Hey!');
  instance.render(document.querySelector('body'));
});
instance.notifyTheOutsideWorld();
```

We brought up a few new concepts. First, we defined a public function—
`notifyTheOutsideWorld`. Ractive.js allows you to register custom methods.
With the `on` method, we subscribed to a specific event, and with `fire`, we
dispatched events.

In the preceding example, we used another method that has not been explained so
far. The `set` function modifies the data object of the component. We will use this
function regularly.

The last thing about Ractive.js that we will mention in this chapter is its function of observing the changes in the component's data properties. The following code demonstrates the observation of the `title` property:

```
var Component = Ractive.extend({
  template: '<div><h1>{{title}}</h1></div>'
});
var instance = new Component();
instance.observe('title', function(value) {
    alert(value);
});
instance.set('title', 'Hello!');
```

The preceding example shows an `alert` window with the `Hello!` text. Let's continue with the process of defining the main application's file, or in other words, the client-side entry point of our social network.

Constructing the entry point of the application

While we were constructing the Gulp setup, we created a task for JavaScript bundling. Browserify needs an entry point to resolve dependencies. We set `frontend/js/app.js`. Similarly, for the backend, we will build our logic around the router. The following code sets two routes and provides a helper function to render the Ractive.js component on the page:

```
// frontend/js/app.js
var Router = require('./lib/Router')();
var Home = require('./controllers/Home');
var currentPage;
var body;

var showPage = function(newPage) {
  if(currentPage) { currentPage.teardown(); }
  currentPage = newPage;
  body.innerHTML = '';
  currentPage.render(body);
}

window.onload = function() {
```

```
    body = document.querySelector('body');

    Router
    .add('home', function() {
      var p = new Home();
      showPage(p);
    })
    .add(function() {
      Router.navigate('home');
    })
    .listen()
    .check();

}
```

We require the `Router` variable at the top. Along with this, we need to fetch the controller responsible for the home page. We will learn more about this in the next section. For now, we will just say that it is a Ractive.js component.

We don't want to run any JavaScript until the resources of the page are fully loaded. So, we will wrap our bootstrapping code in a `window.onload` handler. The holder of the Ractive.js components will be the `body` tag and we will create a reference to it. We defined a helper function called `showPage`. Its job is to render the current page and make sure that the page that was last added is removed properly. The `teardown` method is a built-in function of the framework. It unrenders the component and removes all the event handlers.

For this chapter, we will have only one page — the home page. We will use the router that we created for the backend and register a `/home` route. The second handler that we pass to the `add` function is basically called in case there is no matching route. What we did was immediately forward the user to the `/home` URL. In the end, we triggered the router's listening and fired the initial check.

In the next section, we will define our first controller — the component that will control our home page.

Defining a controller

The role of controllers in our context will be to orchestrate the pages. In other words, they will act as page wrappers that manage the processes that happen between subcomponents. The content of the `controllers/Home.js` file is as follows:

```
module.exports = Ractive.extend({
  template: require('../../tpl/home'),
```

```
    components: {
      navigation: require('../views/Navigation'),
      appfooter: require('../views/Footer')
    },
    onrender: function() {
      console.log('Home page rendered');
    }
  });
```

Before you go through the properties of the template and components, we have to say a few words about `onrender`. The Ractive.js components provide an interface to define handlers for processes that happen internally at each stage of the component's life cycle. For example, we will need to perform some actions almost every time after the component is rendered on the page. Also, there are `onconstruct`, `onteardown`, or `onupdate`. This is surely a nice way to implement business logic. All properties such as these are listed in the official documentation of the framework at `http://docs.ractivejs.org/latest/options`.

We already mentioned the `template` property while introducing you to Ractive.js. However, in the following code we do not have a string as a value. We require another JavaScript file—the precompiled HTML template. The precompilation is done by the build system Gulp in the following way:

```
// gulpfile.js
gulp.task('templates', function() {
  gulp.src('./frontend/tpl/**/*.html')
    .pipe(tap(function(file, t) {
      var precompiled = Ractive.parse(file.contents.toString());
      precompiled = JSON.stringify(precompiled);
      file.contents = new Buffer('module.exports = ' + precompiled);
    }))
    .pipe(rename(function(path) {
      path.extname = '.js';
    }))
    .pipe(gulp.dest('./frontend/tpl'))
});
```

We will get all the HTML files from the `frontend/tpl` directory and convert them to JavaScript files that Ractive.js and Browserify understand. In the end, Gulp creates a file with the same name in the same directory but with a different extension. For example, the template for our home page can be as follows:

```
// frontend/tpl/home.html
<header>
```

```
    <navigation />
    <div class="hero">
      <h1>Node.js by example</h1>
    </div>
  </header>
  <appfooter />
```

When we run `gulp` in the terminal, we will get `frontend/tpl/home.js` with the following content:

```
module.exports =
{"v":1,"t":[{"t":7,"e":"footer","f":["Version:
",{"t":2,"r":"version"}]}]}
```

We do not have to fully understand what these properties mean. The conversion of the JavaScript file to HTML is a job that is reserved for the framework.

If you check the template and component definition in the preceding code, you will notice that there are two subcomponents, `navigation` and `appfooter`. Let's see how to create them.

Managing our views

Again, the views are Ractive.js components. They have their own templates. In fact, the `Home.js` module can also be called a view. The Model-View-Controller pattern in the browser is often transformed, and it does not follow the exact definitions. This is the case with our application because we are using a framework that has some rules and which provides specific functionalities that do not align with the typical MVC. Of course, there is nothing wrong with this. As long as we separate the responsibilities, our architecture will be in good shape.

The `navigation` view is fairly simple. It just defines the template that needs rendering:

```
// views/navigation.js
module.exports = Ractive.extend({
  template: require('../../tpl/navigation')
});
```

In order to make things more interesting and introduce the model's definition, we will display a version number in the footer. This number will come from a model created in `models/Version.js`. Here is the code of the `views/Footer.js` file:

```
var FooterModel = require('../models/Version');

module.exports = Ractive.extend({
  template: require('../../tpl/footer'),
  onrender: function() {
    var model = new FooterModel();
    model.bindComponent(this).fetch();
  }
});
```

Before explaining what exactly happened with `bindComponent`, let's check what we have in `tpl/footer.html`:

```
<footer>
  Version: {{version}}
</footer>
```

We have a dynamic variable, `version`. In case we do not use a model, we have to define it in the `data` property of the component or use `this.set('data', value)`. However, the `FooterModel` module will make our life easier and update the variables of the component that are bound to it. This is why we are passing this module to `bindComponent`. The `fetch` method, as we will see in the next section, synchronizes the model's data with the data in the backend.

Creating a model

We will probably have several models and all of them will share the same methods. Normally, the models make HTTP requests to the server and get data. So, this is something that we need to abstract. Thankfully, Ractive.js makes it possible for you to extend components. Here is the code for the `models/Version.js` file:

```
var Base = require('./Base');
module.exports = Base.extend({
  data: {
    url: '/api/version'
  }
});
```

We have `models/Base.js`, the file that will contain these common functions. It will be a base class that we will later inherit.

```
var ajax = require('../lib/Ajax');
module.exports = Ractive.extend({
  data: {
    value: null,
    url: ''
  },
  fetch: function() {
    var self = this;
    ajax.request({
      url: self.get('url'),
      json: true
    })
    .done(function(result) {
      self.set('value', result);
    })
    .fail(function(xhr) {
      self.fire('Error fetching ' + self.get('url'))
    });
    return this;
  },
  bindComponent: function(component) {
    if(component) {
      this.observe('value', function(v) {
        for(var key in v) {
          component.set(key, v[key]);
            }
      }, { init: false });
    }
    return this;
  }
});
```

We defined two methods — `fetch` and `bindComponent`. The first one uses a helper Ajax wrapper. We are not going to go into the details of this for now. It's similar to jQuery's `.ajax` method and it implements the promise interface pattern. The actual source code can be found in the files that came with this book.

The component that extends the `Base` module should provide a URL. This is the endpoint where the model will make requests. In our case, this is `/api/version`. Our backend will serve content on this URL.

If you go back and check what we did with the URLs starting with /api, we will see that the result is just an empty object. Let's change this and cover the implementation of the /api/version route. We will update backend/API.js as follows:

```
var response = function(result, res) {
  res.writeHead(200, {'Content-Type': 'application/json'});
  res.end(JSON.stringify(result) + '\n');
}
var Router = require('../frontend/js/lib/router')();
Router
.add('api/version', function(req, res) {
  response({
    version: '0.1'
  }, res);
})
.add(function(req, res) {
  response({
    success: true
  }, res);
});

module.exports = function(req, res) {
  Router.check(req.url, [req, res]);
}
```

We used the same router to map the URL to the specific response. So, after this change, our model will fetch 0.1 as a value.

Finally, let's reveal the magic that happens in the bindComponent function:

```
bindComponent: function(component) {
  if(component) {
    this.observe('value', function(v) {
      for(var key in v) component.set(key, v[key]);
    }, { init: false });
  }
  return this;
}
```

We observe the local data property value for changes. It is updated after a successful fetch method call. The new value is passed to the handler and we simply transfer the variables to the component. They are just a few lines of code, but they manage to bring about a nice abstraction. In the actual model definition, we only have to specify the URL. The Base module takes care of the rest.

Summary

In this chapter, we constructed the base of our application. We also created the base of our system—the router. The controllers are now nicely bound to routes and the views are rendered on the page, updating the display automatically when changes are made to the values in the model. We also introduced a simple model that gets data from the backend's API.

In the next chapter, we will implement a real working feature—we will manage the users of our system.

5
Managing Users

In *Chapter 4, Developing the Model-View-Controller Layers,* we used the Model-View-Controller pattern and wrote the base of our social network. We split our application into backend and frontend directories. The code in the first folder serves the assets and generates the home page. Along with this, we made the base of our backend API. The client side of the project is driven by the Ractive.js framework. This is the place where we store our controllers, models, and views. With these elements, we will continue with the management of users. In this part of the book, we will cover the following topics:

- Working with the MongoDB database
- Registering a new user
- User authentication with sessions
- Managing a user's profile

Working with the MongoDB database

Nowadays, almost every web application stores and retrieves data from a database. One of the most popular databases that works well with Node.js is MongoDB (http://www.mongodb.org/). This is what we are going to use. The main characteristic of MongoDB is that it is a NoSQL database with a different data format and query language.

Installing MongoDB

As with every other popular software, MongoDB is available for all operating systems. If you are a Windows user, there is an installer that you can download from the official page `http://www.mongodb.org/downloads`. For Linux or OS X developers, MongoDB is reachable through most popular package management systems. We are not going to cover the installation in detail, but you will find nicely written instructions at `http://docs.mongodb.org/manual/installation/`.

Running MongoDB

After its successful installation, we will have a `mongod` command available. By running it in the terminal, we start a MongoDB server listening by default on port `27017`. Our Node.js backend will connect to this port and execute database queries. Here is how our console looks like after the execution of the `mongod` command:

```
                        1. mongod (mongod)
~
krasimir$ mongod                                                    1 ↵
mongod --help for help and startup options
2014-12-23T00:49:20.622+0200 [initandlisten] MongoDB starting : pid=17452 port=27017
dbpath=/data/db 64-bit host=Krasimirs-MacBook-Pro.local
2014-12-23T00:49:20.622+0200 [initandlisten] db version v2.6.6
2014-12-23T00:49:20.622+0200 [initandlisten] git version: nogitversion
2014-12-23T00:49:20.622+0200 [initandlisten] build info: Darwin miniyosemite.local 14
.0.0 Darwin Kernel Version 14.0.0: Fri Sep 19 00:26:44 PDT 2014; root:xnu-2782.1.97~2
/RELEASE_X86_64 x86_64 BOOST_LIB_VERSION=1_49
2014-12-23T00:49:20.622+0200 [initandlisten] allocator: tcmalloc
2014-12-23T00:49:20.622+0200 [initandlisten] options: {}
2014-12-23T00:49:20.623+0200 [initandlisten] journal dir=/data/db/journal
2014-12-23T00:49:20.623+0200 [initandlisten] recover : no journal files present, no r
ecovery needed
2014-12-23T00:49:20.657+0200 [initandlisten] waiting for connections on port 27017
```

Connecting to the database server

A benefit of Node.js is the existence of thousands of modules. Because of the growing community, we have a module for almost every task that we come across. We have already used several Gulp plugins. Now, we will add the official MongoDB driver to the package.json file:

```
"dependencies": {
  "mongodb": "1.4.25",
  ..
}
```

We have to run npm install to get the module into the node_modules directory. Once the process finishes, we can connect to the server with the following code:

```
var MongoClient = require('mongodb').MongoClient;
MongoClient.connect('mongodb://127.0.0.1:27017/nodejs-by-example',
function(err, db) {
  // ...
});
```

In this code, nodejs-by-example is the name of our database. The callback that is invoked gives us access to the driver's API. We can use the db object to operate with the collections in the database or in other words, create, update, retrieve, or delete documents. This can be demonstrated with the following example:

```
var collection = db.collection('users');
collection.insert({
  name: 'John',
  email: 'john@test.com'
}, function(err, result) {
  // ...
});
```

Now we know how to manage the data in our system. Let's continue to the next section and extend our client-side code.

Extending the code from the previous chapter

Adding new functionalities to the code base that already exists means refactoring and extending the already written code. In order to develop the management of users, we need to update the models/Base.js file. So far, we have a simple Version model and we will need a new User model. An improvement in our navigation and routing is needed so that users have pages to create, edit, and manage their accounts.

The code that comes with this chapter has a lot of additions to the CSS styles. We are not going to discuss them, because we want to focus more on the JavaScript part. They provide a slightly better look to the application. If you are interested in how the final CSS is generated, check out the code pack of this book.

Updating our base model class

So far, models/Base.js has had only two methods. The first one, fetch, performs a GET request to the server with the given URL. In *Chapter 2, Architecting the Project*, we talked about REST APIs; to fully support this architecture, we have to add methods to create, update, and remove records. In fact, all these methods will be close to the one that we already have. Here is the create function:

```
create: function(callback) {
  var self = this;
  ajax.request({
    url: self.get('url'),
    method: 'POST',
    data: this.get('value'),
    json: true
  })
  .done(function(result) {
    if(callback) {
      callback(null, result);
    }
  })
  .fail(function(xhr) {
    if(callback) {
      callback(JSON.parse(xhr.responseText));
    }
  });
  return this;
}
```

We run the method of the model, which gets the data from its `value` property and executes a `POST` request. In the end, we fire a callback. If there is a problem, we send the error as a first argument. If not, then the first argument (representing an error state) is `null` and the second one contains the server's response.

We will follow the same approach for updating and deleting code:

```
save: function(callback) {
  var self = this;
  ajax.request({
    url: self.get('url'),
    method: 'PUT',
    data: this.get('value'),
    json: true
  })
  .done(function(result) { // ...  })
  .fail(function(xhr) { // ... });
  return this;
},
del: function(callback) {
  var self = this;
  ajax.request({
    url: self.get('url'),
    method: 'DELETE',
    json: true
  })
  .done(function(result) { ...  })
  .fail(function(xhr) { ... });
  return this;
}
```

The difference is the `request` method. For the `save` operation, we use `PUT`, and to remove data, we use `DELETE`. Note that during the deletion, we do not have to send the model's data as we are performing a simple operation to remove a specific data object from the database and not making more complex changes as seen in the `create` and `save` requests.

Updating page navigation and routing

The code from *Chapter 4, Developing the Model-View-Controller Layers*, contains only two links in its navigation. We need to add a bit more to it—links to register, log in and out, and profile management access. The `frontend/tpl/navigation.html` template fragment looks like this:

```
<nav>
  <ul>
    <li><a on-click="goto:home">Home</a></li>
    {{#if !isLogged }}
      <li><a on-click="goto:register">Register</a></li>
      <li><a on-click="goto:login">Login</a></li>
    {{else}}
      <li class="right"><a on-click="goto:logout">Logout</a></li>
      <li class="right"><a on-click="goto:profile">Profile</a></li>
    {{/if}}
  </ul>
</nav>
```

Together with the new `<a>` tags, we made the following two interesting additions:

- There is an `{{#if}}` expression. In our Ractive.js component, we need to register an `isLogged` variable. It will control the state of the navigation by hiding and showing the appropriate buttons. When the user is not logged in, we will display the **Register** and **Login** buttons. Otherwise, our application will show the **Logout** and **Profile** links. More about the `isLogged` variable will be discussed at the end of this chapter when we cover session support.

- We have the `on-click` attributes. Note that these attributes are not valid HTML, but they are interpreted by Ractive.js to produce the desired result. Every link in the navigation will dispatch a `goto` event with a specific parameter, and this will happen when the links are triggered by the user.

In the main file of the application (`frontend/js/app.js`), we have a `showPage` function. This method has access to the current page, and it is a perfect place to listen for the `goto` event. It is also a good choice because in the same file, we have a reference to the router. Thus, we are able to change the current site's page. A little change to this function and we are done with the switching of the pages:

```
var showPage = function(newPage) {
  if(currentPage) currentPage.teardown();
  currentPage = newPage;
```

```
body.innerHTML = '';
currentPage.render(body);
currentPage.on('navigation.goto', function(e, route) {
  Router.navigate(route);
});
}
```

In the next section, we will continue with the code that will register a new user in our system.

Registering a new user

To handle the registration of users, we need to update both our frontend and backend code. The client-side part of the application will collect the data and the backend will store it in the database.

Updating the frontend

We updated the navigation and now, if users click on the **Register** link, the app will forward them to a /register route. We have to tweak our router and register a handler in the following way:

```
var Register = require('./controllers/Register');
Router
.add('register', function() {
  var p = new Register();
  showPage(p);
})
```

As with the home page, we will create a new controller located in frontend/js/ controllers/Register.js, as follows:

```
module.exports = Ractive.extend({
  template: require('../../tpl/register'),
  components: {
    navigation: require('../views/Navigation'),
    appfooter: require('../views/Footer')
  },
  onrender: function() {
    var self = this;
    this.observe('firstName',
userModel.setter('value.firstName'));
```

```
    this.observe('lastName', userModel.setter('value.lastName'));
    this.observe('email', userModel.setter('value.email'));
    this.observe('password', userModel.setter('value.password'));
    this.on('register', function() {
      userModel.create(function(error, result) {
        if(error) {
          self.set('error', error.error);
        } else {
          self.set('error', false);
          self.set('success', 'Registration successful.
Click <a href="/login">here</a> to login.');
        }
      });
    });
  }
});
```

The template attached to this controller contains a form with several fields—the first and last name, e-mail, and a password:

```
<header>
  <navigation></navigation>
</header>
<div class="hero">
  <h1>Register</h1>
</div>
<form>
  {{#if error && error != ''}}
    <div class="error">{{error}}</div>
  {{/if}}
  {{#if success && success != ''}}
    <div class="success">{{{success}}}</div>
  {{else}}
    <label for="first-name">First name</label>
    <input type="text" id="first-name" value="{{firstName}}"/>
    <label for="last-name">Last name</label>
    <input type="text" id="last-name" value="{{lastName}}" />
    <label for="email">Email</label>
    <input type="text" id="email" value="{{email}}" />
    <label for="password">Password</label>
    <input type="password" id="password" value="{{password}}" />
    <input type="button" value="register" on-click="register" />
  {{/if}}
</form>
<appfooter />
```

It is worth mentioning that we have placeholders for error and success messages. They are protected with the {{#if}} expressions and are hidden by default. If we, in the controller, set a value to the error or success variables, these hidden div elements will become visible. In order to get the values of the input fields, we will use Ractive.js bindings. By setting value="{{firstName}}", we will create a new variable that will be available in our controller. We can even listen for changes in this variable, as follows:

```
this.observe('firstName', function(value) {
    userModel.set('value.firstName', value);
});
```

The data from the input field should be sent to a model class that communicates with the backend. Since we have several form fields, it makes sense to create a helper that saves us a little writing:

```
this.observe('firstName', userModel.setter('value.firstName'));
```

The setter method returns the same closure that we used in the preceding code:

```
// frontend/js/models/Base.js
setter: function(key) {
  var self = this;
  return function(v) {
    self.set(key, v);
  }
}
```

If we look back and check controllers/Register.js, we will see all the fields from the registration form. In this form, we have a button that dispatches the register event. The controller is subscribed for that event and triggers the create function of the model. Based on the result, we either show an error message or display a registration successful message.

In the preceding code, we used a userModel object. This is an instance of the User class, which extends the models/Base.js file. Here is the code that is stored in frontend/js/models/User.js:

```
var Base = require('./Base');
module.exports = Base.extend({
  data: {
    url: '/api/user'
  }
});
```

We extended the base model. So, we got the `create` and `setter` functions automatically. For the registration process, we do not need any other custom methods. However, to log in and out, we will add more functions.

Several parts of our system will need this model. So, we will create its global `userModel` instance. An appropriate place for this is the `frontend/js/app.js` file. The listener of the `window.onload` event is a good host for such code:

```
window.onload = function() {
  ...
  userModel = new UserModel();
  ...
};
```

Note that we missed the `var` keyword in front of the variable definition. This is how we make `userModel` available in the global scope.

Updating the backend API

We have our client-side code making a POST request to the backend with the new user's data. To close the circle, we have to handle the request in our backend API and record the information in the database. Let's first extend `backend/API.js` with a few helper functions and variables:

```
var MongoClient = require('mongodb').MongoClient;
var database;
var getDatabaseConnection = function(callback) {
  if(database) {
    callback(database);
    return;
  } else {
    MongoClient.connect('mongodb://127.0.0.1:27017/nodejs-by-example',
      function(err, db) {
        if(err) {
          throw err;
        };
        database = db;
        callback(database);
      });
  }
};
```

At the beginning of this chapter, we learned how to make queries to the MongoDB database. What we need is access to the driver's API. There is a piece of code that we will use often. So, it is a good idea to wrap it in a helper method. The `getDatabaseConnection` function is exactly the function that can be used to achieve this. It only connects to the database during the first time of its execution. Every call after that returns the cached `database` object.

Another common task typical to Node.js request handling is the fetching of the POST data. The GET parameters are available in the `request` object that comes to every route handler. However, for the POST data, we need a special helper:

```
var querystring = require('querystring');
var processPOSTRequest = function(req, callback) {
  var body = '';
  req.on('data', function (data) {
    body += data;
  });
  req.on('end', function () {
    callback(querystring.parse(body));
  });
};
```

We use the `request` object as a stream and subscribe to its `data` event. Once we receive all the information, we use `querystring.parse` to format it into a usable hashmap (key/value of the POST parameters) object and fire the callback.

In the end, we will add an e-mail validation function. We will need it during the registration and the updating of the user's profile. The actual validation is done with the regular expression:

```
var validEmail = function(value) {
  var re = /^(([^<>()[\]\\.,;:\s@\"]+(\.[^<>()
[\]\\.,;:\s@\"]+)*)|(\".+\"))@(
(\[[0-9]{1,3}\.[0-9]{1,3}\.[0-9]{1,3}\.[0-9]{1,3}\])|(([a-zA-Z\-0-
9]+\.)+[a-zA-Z]{2,}))$/;
  return re.test(value);
};
```

Now let's continue with the code that will accept the POST request and register a new user in the database. So far, we have only added two routes to the API—/api/version and the default one. We will add one more, /api/user, as follows:

```
Router.add('api/user', function(req, res) {
    switch(req.method) {
        case 'GET':
            // ...
        break;
        case 'PUT':
            // ...
        break;
        case 'POST':
            processPOSTRequest(req, function(data) {
                if(!data.firstName || data.firstName === '') {
                    error('Please fill your first name.', res);
                } else if(!data.lastName || data.lastName === '') {
                    error('Please fill your last name.', res);
                } else if(!data.email || data.email === '' ||
                    !validEmail(data.email)) {
                    error('Invalid or missing email.', res);
                } else if(!data.password || data.password === '') {
                    error('Please fill your password.', res);
                } else {
                    getDatabaseConnection(function(db) {
                        var collection = db.collection('users');
                        data.password = sha1(data.password);
                        collection.insert(data, function(err, docs) {
                            response({
                                success: 'OK'
                            }, res);
                        });
                    });
                }
            });
        break;
        case 'DELETE':
            // ...
        break;
    };
});
```

The same route will host different operations. To distinguish them, we will rely on the `request` method as it is described in the REST API concept.

In the `POST` case, we will first fetch the data by using the `processPOSTRequest` helper. After that, we will run a series of checks to make sure that the data sent is correct. If it is not, we will respond with an appropriate error message. If everything is okay, we will use the other `getDatabaseConnection` helper and make a new record in the database. It's not a good practice to store the users' password as plain text. So, before sending them to MongoDB, we will encrypt them using the `sha1` module. This is a module that is available in the Node.js package manager registry. At the top of `backend/API.js`, we will add the following:

```
var sha1 = require('sha1');
```

To get this line working, we have to update the `package.json` file and run `npm install` in the console.

In the next section, we will implement the `GET`, `PUT` and `DELETE` cases. Together with this, we will introduce you to a new route to log in.

User authentication with sessions

We implemented the functionalities that register new users in our system. The next step is to authenticate these users. Let's first provide an interface to enter a username and password. We need to add a new route handler in `frontend/js/app.js`:

```
Router
.add('login', function() {
    var p = new Login();
    showPage(p);
})
```

All the other pages so far use the same idea. We will initialize a new controller and pass it to the `showPage` helper. The template that is used here is as follows:

```
// frontend/tpl/login.html
<header>
  <navigation></navigation>
</header>
<div class="hero">
  <h1>Login</h1>
</div>
<form>
```

```
  {{#if error && error != ''}}
    <div class="error">{{error}}</div>
  {{/if}}
  {{#if success && success != ''}}
    <div class="success">{{{success}}}</div>
  {{else}}
    <label for="email">Email</label>
    <input type="text" id="email" value="{{email}}" />
    <label for="password">Password</label>
    <input type="password" id="password" value="{{password}}" />
    <input type="button" value="login" on-click="login" />
  {{/if}}
</form>
<appfooter />
```

During the registration process, we used similar placeholders for the error and success messages. Again, we have an HTML form. However this time, the form contains input fields for the username and password. We will also bind two variables and make sure that the button dispatches the login event. Here is the code for our controller:

```
// frontend/js/controllers/Login.js
module.exports = Ractive.extend({
  template: require('../../tpl/login'),
  components: {
    navigation: require('../views/Navigation'),
    appfooter: require('../views/Footer')
  },
  onrender: function() {
    var self = this;
    this.observe('email', userModel.setter('email'));
    this.observe('password', userModel.setter('password'));
    this.on('login', function() {
      userModel.login(function(error, result) {
        if(error) {
          self.set('error', error.error);
        } else {
          self.set('error', false);
          // redirecting the user to the home page
          window.location.href = '/';
        }
      });
    });
  }
});
```

By using the same `setter` function, we stored the values filled into our model. There is a `userModel.login` method that is similar to `userModel.create`. It triggers a POST request to the server with the given data. In this case, the data is the username and password. This time, we are not going to use functions from the base model. We will register a new one in the `/frontend/js/models/User.js` file:

```
var ajax = require('../lib/Ajax');
var Base = require('./Base');
module.exports = Base.extend({
  data: {
    url: '/api/user'
  },
  login: function(callback) {
    var self = this;
    ajax.request({
      url: this.get('url') + '/login',
      method: 'POST',
      data: {
        email: this.get('email'),
        password: this.get('password')
      },
      json: true
    })
    .done(function(result) {
      callback(null, result);
    })
    .fail(function(xhr) {
      callback(JSON.parse(xhr.responseText));
    });
  }
});
```

Again, we used the Ajax helper to send information to the backend API. The request goes to the `/api/user/login` URL. At the moment, we will not handle such routes. The following code goes to `/backend/API.js` just above the `/api/user` handler:

```
.add('api/user/login', function(req, res) {
  processPOSTRequest(req, function(data) {
    if(!data.email || data.email === '' ||
!validEmail(data.email)) {
      error('Invalid or missing email.', res);
    } else if(!data.password || data.password === '') {
      error('Please enter your password.', res);
    } else {
```

```
      getDatabaseConnection(function(db) {
        var collection = db.collection('users');
        collection.find({
          email: data.email,
          password: sha1(data.password)
        }).toArray(function(err, result) {
          if(result.length === 0) {
            error('Wrong email or password', res);
          } else {
            var user = result[0];
            delete user._id;
            delete user.password;
            req.session.user = user;
            response({
              success: 'OK',
              user: user
            }, res);
          }
        });
      });
    }
  });
})
```

The `processPOSTRequest` function delivers the `POST` data sent by the frontend. We will keep the same e-mail and password validation mechanisms. If everything is okay, we will check whether the provided credentials match some of the accounts in the database. The result for a correct e-mail and password is an object containing the user's details. It is not a good idea to return the ID and password of the user. So, we will remove them from the returned user object. There is one more thing that we haven't talked about so far:

```
req.session.user = user;
```

This is how we store a session. By default, we do not have a `session` object available. There is a module that delivers this functionality. It's called `cookie-session`. We have to add it to `package.json` and run the `npm install` command in the terminal. After its successful installation, we have to tweak the `server.js` file:

```
Router
.add('static', Assets)
.add('api', API)
.add(Default);
```

```
var session = require('cookie-session');
var checkSession = function(req, res) {
  session({
    keys: ['nodejs-by-example']
  })(req, res, function() {
    process(req, res);
  });
}
var process = function(req, res) {
  Router.check(req.url, [req, res]);
}
var app = http.createServer(checkSession).listen(port,
'127.0.0.1');
console.log("Listening on 127.0.0.1:" + port);
```

Before passing the application's flow to the router, we run the `checkSession`
function. The method uses the newly added module and patches the `request` object
by attaching the `session` object. All API methods have access to the current's user
session. This means that we may secure every request to the backend by simply
checking whether the user is authenticated or not.

You may remember that at the beginning of this chapter, we created a global
`userModel` object. It's initialization occurred in the `window.onload` handler, which is
effectively the bootstrapping point of our frontend. We can ask the backend whether
the current user is logged in before showing the UI. This will help us display the
proper navigation buttons. So, here is how `frontend/js/app.js` changes:

```
window.onload = function() {
  userModel = new UserModel();
  userModel.fetch(function(error, result) {
    // ... router setting
  });
}
```

The `userModel` function extends the base model where the `fetch` method puts the
response from the server in the `value` property of the model. Fetching data from the
frontend means making a GET request, and in this case, this is a GET request to the
`/api/user` URL. Let's see how `backend/API.js` handles the query:

```
.add('api/user', function(req, res) {
  switch(req.method) {
    case 'GET':
      if(req.session && req.session.user) {
```

```
        response(req.session.user, res);
    } else {
        response({}, res);
    }
    break;
...
```

If the user is logged in, we return what is stored in the `session` object. If not, the backend responds with an empty object. For the client side, this means that the `userModel` object may or may not have information in its `value` property based on the current user's status. So, it makes sense to add a new `isLogin` method in the `frontend/js/models/User.js` file:

```
isLogged: function() {
    return this.get('value.firstName') &&
this.get('value.lastName');
}
```

Adding the preceding function, we can use the `userModel.isLogged()` call anywhere in our client-side code and we will know whether the user has logged in or not. This will work because we performed the fetching at the very beginning of our application. For example, the navigation (`frontend/js/views/Navigation.js`) needs this information in order to display the correct links:

```
module.exports = Ractive.extend({
    template: require('../../tpl/navigation'),
    onconstruct: function() {
        this.data.isLogged = userModel.isLogged();
    }
});
```

Managing a user's profile

The previous sections of this chapter gave us enough knowledge to update the information saved in the database. Again, we need to create a page in the frontend that has an HTML form. The difference here is that the input fields of the form should be filled by default with the data of the current user. So, let's start by adding a route handler for the `/profile` URL:

```
Route
.add('profile', function() {
    if(userModel.isLogged()) {
        var p = new Profile();
```

```
      showPage(p);
   } else {
      Router.navigate('login');
   }
})
```

There is no reason to allow access to this page if the user is not logged in. A simple authentication check before calling the `showPage` helper forwards the user to the login page if needed.

The template that we need for the `Profile` controller is identical to the one that we used for registration. There are only two things that we have to change—we need to remove the `email` field and update the label of the button from **Register** to **Update**. The removing of the `email` field is not absolutely necessary, but it is a good practice to prevent changes by the user and leave it as it was entered during the registration. Here is how the controller looks:

```
module.exports = Ractive.extend({
   template: require('../../tpl/profile'),
   components: {
      navigation: require('../views/Navigation'),
      appfooter: require('../views/Footer')
   },
   onrender: function() {
      var self = this;
      this.set(userModel.get('value'));
      this.on('updateProfile', function() {
         userModel.set('value.firstName', this.get('firstName'));
         userModel.set('value.lastName', this.get('lastName'));
         if(this.get('password') != '') {
            userModel.set('value.password', this.get('password'));
         }
         userModel.save(function(error, result) {
            if(error) {
               self.set('error', error.error);
            } else {
               self.set('error', false);
               self.set('success', 'Profile updated successfully.');
            }
         });
      });
   }
});
```

The `updateProfile` event is the event that is fired by the button on the page. We update the `model` fields with the values from the form. The password is changed only if the user enters something in the field. Otherwise, the backend keeps the old value.

We will call `userModel.save`, which performs a PUT request to the API. Here is how we handle the request in `backend/API.js`:

```
.add('api/user', function(req, res) {
  switch(req.method) {
    case 'PUT':
      processPOSTRequest(req, function(data) {
        if(!data.firstName || data.firstName === '') {
          error('Please fill your first name.', res);
        } else if(!data.lastName || data.lastName === '') {
          error('Please fill your last name.', res);
        } else {
          getDatabaseConnection(function(db) {
            var collection = db.collection('users');
            if(data.password) {
              data.password = sha1(data.password);
            }
            collection.update(
              { email: req.session.user.email },
              { $set: data },
              function(err, result) {
                if(err) {
                  err('Error updating the data.');
                } else {
                  if(data.password) delete data.password;
                  for(var key in data) {
                    req.session.user[key] = data[key];
                  }
                  response({
                    success: 'OK'
                  }, res);
                }
              }
            );
          });
        }
      });
      break;
```

The usual field validation is here again. We will check whether the user has typed something for their first and last name. The password is updated only if there is data for the same. It's important to note that we need the user's e-mail to update the profile. This is how we refer to the exact record in our MongoDB database. Since we stored the e-mail in the session of the user, it is quite easy to fetch it from there. If everything goes well, we update the information in the `session` object. This is needed because the frontend gets the user's details from there, and if we forget to perform this change, our UI will show the old data.

Summary

In this chapter, we made a lot of progress. We built one of the core features of our social network — user management. We learned how to store data in a MongoDB database and use sessions to authenticate users.

In the next chapter, we will implement the functions of friend management. The users of any social network will be familiar with the same. At the end of the next chapter, users will be able to make friends using our application.

6
Adding Friendship Capabilities

In *Chapter 5, Managing Users*, we implemented the user registration and login system. We now have user information in our database and we can continue with one of the most important characteristics of social networks — friendship. In this chapter, we will add a logic for the following:

- Finding friends
- Marking users as friends
- Displaying the linked users on the **Profile** page

Finding friends

The process of finding friends involves a series of changes in our current codebase. The following sections will guide us through the searching and displaying of friend profiles. We will make a couple of improvements in our REST API and define a new controller and model.

Adding the search page

So far, we have pages for registration, login, and profile management. We will add one more link in our navigation — Find friends. In order to do this, we have to update the frontend/tpl/navigation.html file as follows:

```
<li class="right"><a on-click="goto:logout">Logout</a></li>
<li class="right"><a on-click="goto:profile">Profile</a></li>
<li class="right"><a on-click="goto:find-friends">Find
friends</a></li>
```

The link that we added at the end will forward the user to a new route. As with the other pages, our router will catch the URL change and fire a handler. Here is a little update of the app.js file:

```
Router
.add('find-friends', function() {
  if(userModel.isLogged()) {
    var p = new FindFriends();
    showPage(p);
  } else {
    Router.navigate('login');
  }
})
```

The adding of new friends should not be possible if the user is not authenticated. We will apply a simple check here in the frontend, but we will protect the API calls too. A new FindFriends controller has to be created. The role of this controller is to show a form with an input field and a button. The user submits the form, we query the database, and we later display the users that match the entered string. Here is how the controller begins:

```
// frontend/js/controllers/FindFriends.js
module.exports = Ractive.extend({
  template: require('../../tpl/find-friends'),
  components: {
    navigation: require('../views/Navigation'),
    appfooter: require('../views/Footer')
  },
  data: {
    loading: false,
    message: '',
    searchFor: '',
    foundFriends: null
  },
  onrender: function() {
    // ...
  }
});
```

We kept the same `Navigation` and `Footer` components. There are several variables with their respective default values. The `loading` keyword will be used as a flag indicating that we are making a request to the API. The fetching of friends that match certain criteria may be a complex operation. So, it will be a good practice to show the user that we are working on his/her query. The `message` property will be used either to display confirmation that everything went okay or to report an error. The last two variables keep the data. The `searchFor` variable will host the string entered by the user and `foundFriends` will host the users returned by the backend.

Let's check what we need as the HTML markup. The `frontend/tpl/find-friends.html` file contains the following:

```
<header>
  <navigation></navigation>
</header>
<div class="hero">
  <h1>Find friends</h1>
</div>
<form onsubmit="return false;">
  {{#if loading}}
    <p>Loading. Please wait.</p>
  {{else}}
    <label for="friend-name">
      Please, type the name of your friend:
    </label>
    <input type="text" id="friend-name" value="{{friendName}}"/>
    <input type="button" value="Find" on-click="find" />
  {{/if}}
</form>
{{#if foundFriends !== null}}
  <div class="friends-list">
    {{#each foundFriends}}
      <div class="friend-list-item">
        <h2>{{firstName}} {{lastName}}</h2>
        <input type="button" value="Add as a friend"
        on-click="add:{{id}}"/>
      </div>
    {{/each}}
  </div>
{{/if}}
```

```
{{#if message !== ''}}
  <div class="friends-list">
    <p>{{{message}}}</p>
  </div>
{{/if}}
<appfooter />
```

The `header` and the `navigation` sections stay untouched. We have a nicely placed title at the top followed by the form that we mentioned. If the `loading` flag has `true` as a value, we display the **Loading. Please wait.** message. If we are not in the process of querying the backend, then we show the input field and the button. The following screenshot demonstrates how this looks in practice:

The next part of the template renders the users sent by the backend. It shows their name and a **Add as a friend** button. We will see a screenshot of this view in the pages that follow.

The last part of the HTML markup is for the conditional displaying of a message. If we set a value to the `message` variable, then Ractive.js reveals the `div` element and makes our text visible.

Writing the model

We have the user interface that will accept the user's input. Now, we need to communicate with the backend and retrieve users matching the value of the form's field. In our system, we make requests to the API through models.

So, let's create a new `frontend/js/models/Friends.js` model:

```
var ajax = require('../lib/Ajax');
var Base = require('./Base');

module.exports = Base.extend({
  data: {
    url: '/api/friends'
  },
  find: function(searchFor, callback) {
    ajax.request({
      url: this.get('url') + '/find',
      method: 'POST',
      data: {
        searchFor: searchFor
      },
      json: true
    })
    .done(function(result) {
      callback(null, result);
    })
    .fail(function(xhr) {
      callback(JSON.parse(xhr.responseText));
    });
  }
});
```

The endpoint of the `friendship` functionality will be `/api/friends`. To search among users, we append `/find` to the URL. We are going to make a POST request with the value of the `searchFor` variable. The code that handles the result again uses the `lib/Ajax` module, and if everything is okay, it fires the specified callback.

Let's update the controller that calls the newly created model and its `find` function. At the top of the `controllers/FindFriends.js` file, we will add a `require` statement:

```
var Friends = require('../models/Friends');
```

Then, in the `render` handler of the controller, we will place the following snippet:

```
onrender: function() {

  var model = new Friends();
  var self = this;
```

```
this.on('find', function(e) {
  self.set('loading', true);
  self.set('message', '');
  var searchFor = this.get('friendName');
  model.find(searchFor, function(err, res) {

    if(res.friends && res.friends.length > 0) {
      self.set('foundFriends', res.friends);
    } else {
      self.set('foundFriends', null);
      self.set('message', 'Sorry, there is no friends matching
      <strong>' + searchFor + '<strong>');
    }
    self.set('loading', false);
  });
});


}
```

The `find` event is fired by the button in our form. Once we register the button's click, we display the `loading` string and clear any previously shown message. We get the value of the input field and ask the model for matching users. If there are any such potential friends, we render them by setting a value to the `foundFriends` variable. If not, we display a message saying that there are no users who match the criteria. Once we finish with the API method implementation, the screen will look like this:

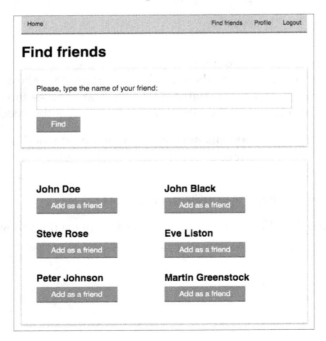

Fetching friends from the database

The changes that we need to make are in `backend/API.js`. We need to add a couple of new routes. However, before proceeding with the querying of users, we will add a helper function to fetch the current user's profile. We will keep the name and e-mail of the current user in a `session` variable, but that's not enough, because we want to display more user information. So, the following function fetches the complete profile from the database:

```
var getCurrentUser = function(callback, req, res) {
  getDatabaseConnection(function(db) {
    var collection = db.collection('users');
    collection.find({
      email: req.session.user.email
    }).toArray(function(err, result) {
      if(result.length === 0) {
        error('No such user', res);
      } else {
        callback(result[0]);
      }
    });
  });
};
```

We use the e-mail of the user as a criterion for the request. The object containing the profile's data is returned as an argument of the callback.

Since we have all the information about the current user, we can continue implementing the user's search. The route that should answer such queries is as follows:

```
Router
.add('api/friends/find', function(req, res) {
  if(req.session && req.session.user) {
    if(req.method === 'POST') {
      processPOSTRequest(req, function(data) {
        getDatabaseConnection(function(db) {
          getCurrentUser(function(user) {
            findFriends(db, data.searchFor, user.friends || []);
          }, req, res);
        });
      });
    });
```

```
      } else {
        error('This method accepts only POST requests.', res);
      }
    } else {
      error('You must be logged in to use this method.', res);
    }
  })
```

The first `if` clause guarantees that this route is accessible only to the registered and logged in users. This method accepts only the `POST` requests. The rest fetches the `searchFor` variable and calls the `findFriends` function, which can be implemented as follows:

```
var findFriends = function(db, searchFor, currentFriends) {
  var collection = db.collection('users');
  var regExp = new RegExp(searchFor, 'gi');
  var excludeEmails = [req.session.user.email];
  currentFriends.forEach(function(value, index, arr) {
    arr[index] = ObjectId(value);
  });
  collection.find({
    $and: [
      {
        $or: [
          { firstName: regExp },
          { lastName: regExp }
        ]
      },
      { email: { $nin: excludeEmails } },
      { _id: { $nin: currentFriends } }
    ]
  }).toArray(function(err, result) {
    var foundFriends = [];
    for(var i=0; i<result.length; i++) {
      foundFriends.push({
        id: result[i]._id,
        firstName: result[i].firstName,
        lastName: result[i].lastName
      });
    };
    response({
      friends: foundFriends
    }, res);
  });
}
```

The users in our system have their names split into two variables — `firstName` and `lastName`. We cannot be sure as to which one the user may be referring to when they type in the search form's field. So, we will search in the database of both properties. We will also use a regular expression to make sure that our search is not case-sensitive.

The MongoDB database provides a syntax to perform complex queries. In our case, we want to fetch the following:

- The users whose first or last names match the criteria sent by the client side.
- The users who are different from the already added friends of the current user.
- The users who are different from the current user. We don't want to offer the friendship of the user with their own profile.

The `$nin` variable means *value not in the provided array*. We will exclude the e-mail address of the current user. A little detail that is worth a mention is that MongoDB stores the IDs of the users in a 12-byte BSON type. They are not in plain text. So, we need to use a `ObjectID` function before sending the query. The method is accessible via the same `mongodb` module — `var ObjectId = require('mongodb').ObjectID`.

When the database driver returns the records that fulfill our criteria, we filter the information and respond with a proper JSON file. We will not send the entire profiles of the users, because we are not going to use all the data. The names and IDs are enough.

Adding that new route to the API will make friend searching work. Now, let's add logic that attaches profiles to the current user.

Marking users as friends

If we check the HTML template of our new page, we will see that every rendered user has a button that dispatches an `add` event. Let's handle this in our controller and run a function in our model, which is similar to the process of finding friends:

```
this.on('add', function(e, id) {
  this.set('loading', true);
  model.add(id, function(err, res) {
    self.set('foundFriends', null);
    if(err) {
      self.set('message', 'Operation failed.');
    } else if(res.success === 'OK') {
```

```
      self.set('message', 'Operation successful.');
    }
    self.set('loading', false);
  });
});
```

We use the same technique with the `loading` flag. The model's method that we will cover in the following code accepts the `id` value of the user and reports if the linking is successful. We need to clear the `foundFriends` array. Otherwise, the current user may click on the same profile twice. The other option is to remove only the clicked item, but this involves more code.

The addition in `models/Friends.js` is as follows:

```
add: function(id, callback) {
  ajax.request({
    url: this.get('url') + '/add',
    method: 'POST',
    data: {
      id: id
    },
    json: true
  })
  .done(function(result) {
    callback(null, result);
  })
  .fail(function(xhr) {
    callback(JSON.parse(xhr.responseText));
  });
}
```

The only difference between the `add` and `find` methods is that in the first one, we sent `searchFor` and in the second one, we sent the `id` parameter. The error handling and result responding is the same. Of course, the endpoints are also tweaked.

We show profiles, the user clicks on some of them, and our model fires a POST request to the backend. It is time to implement the API route that marks users as friends. To do this, we will update the current user's profile by adding a new array called `friends`, which contains references to friends' profiles:

```
.add('api/friends/add', function(req, res) {
  if(req.session && req.session.user) {
    if(req.method === 'POST') {
```

```
        var friendId;
        var updateUserData = function(db, friendId) {
          var collection = db.collection('users');
          collection.update(
            { email: req.session.user.email },
            { $push: { friends: friendId } },
            done
          );
        };
        var done = function(err, result) {
          if(err) {
            error('Error updating the data.', res);
          } else {
            response({
              success: 'OK'
            }, res);
          }
        };
        processPOSTRequest(req, function(data) {
          getDatabaseConnection(function(db) {
            updateUserData(db, data.id);
          });
        });
      } else {
        error('This method accepts only POST requests.', res);
      }
    } else {
      error('You must be logged in to use this method.', res);
    }
  }
})
```

The preceding method is again protected. We require an authenticated user and a POST request to be made. After fetching the ID of the friend, we use the $push operator to create (if it doesn't exist) and fill the friends array. The only job of the done function is to send a response to the browser.

Our next step in this chapter is to show the added friends on the **Profile** page of the user.

Displaying the linked users on the Profile page

Again, we'll start by updating our templates. In the previous chapter, we created `frontend/tpl/profile.html`. It contains a form that we use for profile updates. Let's add the following code after it:

```
{{#if friends.length > 0}}
  <div class="hero">
    <h1>Friends</h1>
  </div>
  <div class="friends-list">
    {{#each friends:index}}
      <div class="friend-list-item">
        <h2>{{friends[index].firstName}}
{{friends[index].lastName}}</h2>
      </div>
    {{/each}}
  </div>
{{/if}}
```

If the Ractive component has a `friends` property, then we will render a list of users. The page will display the name of the users and it will look like the next screenshot:

The controller that renders the page should also be updated. We should use the same `models/Friends` model that was developed in the previous sections. This is why we need to add `var Friends = require('../models/Friends');` at the top. Three other lines of code will make the fetching of records work. We will add them in the `onrender` handler of the controller as follows:

```
// controllers/Profile.js
onrender: function() {

    ...

    var friends = new Friends();
    friends.fetch(function(err, result) {
      self.set('friends', result.friends);    });
}
```

Another small addition that we have to make in the controller is defining a default value of the `friends` variable, which is as follows:

```
data: {
  friends: []
},
onrender: function() {
  ...
}
```

This time, we are not going to update the model. We will use the default `fetch` method that sends a GET request to the `/api/friends` endpoint. The only addition that needs to be made is in the `backend/API.js` file. We need a route that finds the friends of the current user and returns them:

```
.add('api/friends', function(req, res) {
  if(req.session && req.session.user) {
    getCurrentUser(function(user) {
      if(!user.friends || user.friends.length === 0) {
        return response({ friends: [] }, res);
      }
      user.friends.forEach(function(value, index, arr) {
        arr[index] = ObjectId(value);
      });
      getDatabaseConnection(function(db) {
        var collection = db.collection('users');
        collection.find({
```

```
            _id: { $in: user.friends }
        }).toArray(function(err, result) {
          result.forEach(function(value, index, arr) {
            arr[index].id = value.id;
              delete arr[index].password;
              delete arr[index].email;
              delete arr[index]._id;
          });
          response({
            friends: result
          }, res);
        });
      });
    }, req, res);
  } else {
    error('You must be logged in to use this method.', res);
  }
})
```

This is the second place that we used the `getCurrentUser` helper function.
We do not have the profiles of the users. So, we need to make one additional request
to the MongoDB server. The `$in` operator helps us in this case. Again, we need to
convert the IDs to the proper format before sending them along with the query. In
the end, before responding to the browser, we delete sensitive information, such as
the ID, password, and e-mail. The frontend receives a nice array with all the friends
of the currently logged in user.

Summary

In this chapter, we made the creating of links between users possible. We reinforced
our knowledge about frontend controllers and models. We extended the project's
API with a couple of new methods and performed some complex database queries.

In the next chapter, we will learn how to upload content with Node.js. Like other
popular social networks, the posted information will be shown as a feed to the users.

7
Posting Content

Chapter 6, *Adding Friendship Capabilities*, was about adding friendship capabilities. The ability to connect with other users in a social network is important. However, it is even more important to provide an interface to generate content. In this chapter, we will implement the logic behind content creation. We will cover the following topics:

- Posting and storing text
- Showing the user's feed
- Posting files

Posting and storing text

As in the previous chapters, we have a feature that requires changes in both the frontend and backend parts of our application. We will need an HTML form that accepts the user's text, a new model that handles the communication with the backend, and of course, changes in the API. Let's start by updating our home page.

Adding a form to post text messages

We have a home page that displays a simple title. Let's use it and add a `<textarea>` tag to send content to the API. Later in this chapter, we will use the same page to display the user's feed. Let's replace the lonely `<h1>` tag with the following markup:

```
{{#if posting === true}}
  <form enctype="multipart/form-data" method="post">
    <h3>What is on your mind?</h3>
    {{#if error && error != ''}}
      <div class="error">{{{error}}}</div>
    {{/if}}
```

```
    {{#if success && success != ''}}
      <div class="success">{{{success}}}</div>
    {{/if}}
    <label for="text">Text</label>
    <textarea value="{{text}}"></textarea>
    <input type="file" name="file" />
    <input type="button" value="Post" on-click="post" />
  </form>
{{else}}
  <h1>Node.js by example</h1>
{{/if}}
```

We still have the heading there, but it is displayed only if the `posting` variable is equal to `false`. In the next section, where we will update the controller of the home page, we will use `posting` to protect the content's form. In some cases, we do not want to make `<textarea>` visible.

Note that we have two blocks to show messages. The first one will be visible if there is an error during the posting and the second one when everything goes well. The rest of the form is the needed user interface—the text area, input file field, and a button. The button dispatches a post event that we will catch in the controller.

Introducing the content's model

We will definitely need a model to manage communication with the API. Let's create a new `models/Content.js` file and place the following code there:

```
var ajax = require('../lib/Ajax');
var Base = require('./Base');

module.exports = Base.extend({
  data: {
    url: '/api/content'
  },
  create: function(content, callback) {
    var self = this;
    ajax.request({
      url: this.get('url'),
      method: 'POST',
      data: {
```

```
      text: content.text
    },
    json: true
  })
  .done(function(result) {
    callback(null, result);
  })
  .fail(function(xhr) {
    callback(JSON.parse(xhr.responseText));
  });
}
});
```

The module extends the same `models/Base.js` class, which is similar to the other models in our system. The `lib/Ajax.js` module is needed because we are going to make HTTP requests. We should be familiar with the rest of the code. A POST request to `/api/content` is made by sending text that is passed as an argument to the `create` function.

The module will be updated when we reach the file posting. To create records that are based only on text, this is enough.

Updating the controller of the home page

Now that we have a proper model and form, we are ready to tweak the controller of the home page. As mentioned earlier, the `posting` variable controls the visibility of the form. Its value will be set to `true` by default, and if the user is not logged in, we will change it to `false`. Every Ractive.js component may have a `data` property. It represents the initial state of all the internal variables:

```
// controllers/Home.js
module.exports = Ractive.extend({
  template: require('../../tpl/home'),
  components: {
    navigation: require('../views/Navigation'),
    appfooter: require('../views/Footer')
  },
  data: {
    posting: true
  }
});
```

Now, let's add some logic to the `onrender` handler. This is the entry point to our component. We will start by checking whether the current user is logged in:

```
onrender: function() {
  if(userModel.isLogged()) {
    // ...
  } else {
    this.set('posting', false);
  }
}
```

From *Chapter 5, Managing Users*, we know that `userModel` is a global object that we can use to check the state of the current user. As mentioned earlier, if we have an unauthorized visitor, we have to set `posting` to `false`.

The next logical step is to process the content from the form and submit a request to the API. We will use the newly created `ContentModel` class, as follows:

```
var ContentModel = require('../models/Content');
var model = new ContentModel();
var self = this;
this.on('post', function() {
  model.create({
    text: this.get('text')
  }, function(error, result) {
    self.set('text', '');
    if(error) {
      self.set('error', error.error);
    } else {
      self.set('error', false);
      self.set('success', 'The post is saved successfully.<br />What
        about adding another one?');
    }
  });
});
```

Once the user presses the button in the form, our component dispatches a `post` event. We will then catch the event and call the `create` method of the model. It is important to give a proper response to the user, so we clear the text field with `self.set('text', '')` and use the local `error` and `success` variables to indicate the status of the request.

Storing content in the database

So far, we have an HTML form that submits an HTTP request to the API. In this section, we will update our API so that we can store text content in the database. The endpoint of our model is `/api/content`. We will add a new route and protect it by allowing access to only authorized users:

```
// backend/API.js
.add('api/content', function(req, res) {
  var user;
  if(req.session && req.session.user) {
    user = req.session.user;
  } else {
    error('You must be logged in in order to use this method.', res);
  }
})
```

We will create a `user` local variable that contains the visitor's session data. Every post that goes to the database should have an owner. So, it is good to have a shortcut to the user's profile.

The same `/api/content` directory will be used to fetch the posts too. Again, we will use the `req.method` property to find out what kind of request is coming. If it is GET, we need to fetch the posts from the database and send them to the browser. If it is POST, we have to create a new entry. Here is the code that sends the user's text to the database:

```
switch(req.method) {
  case 'POST':
    processPOSTRequest(req, function(data) {
      if(!data.text || data.text === '') {
        error('Please add some text.', res);
      } else {
        getDatabaseConnection(function(db) {
          getCurrentUser(function(user) {
            var collection = db.collection('content');
            data.userId = user._id.toString();
            data.userName = user.firstName + ' ' + user.lastName;
            data.date = new Date();
            collection.insert(data, function(err, docs) {
              response({
```

```
                      success: 'OK'
                 }, res);
              });
           }, req, res);
        });
      }
    });
  break;
};
```

The data sent by the browser is coming as POST variables. Again, we need the help of
processPOSTRequest to access it. If there is no .text or it is empty, the API returns
an error. If everything is okay and the text message is available, we proceed with
the establishing of the database connection. We also fetch the entire profile of the
current user. The posts in our social network will be saved along with the following
additional properties:

- userId: This represents the creator of the record. We will use this property
  during the feed generation.

- userName: We do not want to call getCurrentUser for every single post that
  we display. So, the name of the owner is directly stored along with the text.
  It is worth mentioning that in some cases, such calls are needed. For example,
  the calls will be needed while changing the name of the user.

- date: We should know the date of the creation of data. It is useful for the
  sorting or filtering of data.

In the end, we call collection.insert, which effectively stores the entry in
the database.

In the next section, we will see how to retrieve created content and display it to
the user.

Showing the user's feed

Now, every user is able to store messages in our database. Let's continue by showing
the records in the browser. We will start by adding logic to the API that fetches the
posts. It will be interesting because you should get the messages sent by not only a
specific user, but also to his/her friends. We used the POST method to create content.
The following lines will process the GET requests.

First, we will get the IDs of the user's friends in the following way:

```
case 'GET':
  getCurrentUser(function(user) {
    if(!user.friends) {
      user.friends = [];
    }
    // ...
  break;
```

In the previous chapter, we implemented friendship capabilities and kept the IDs of the user's friends directly in the profile of the user. The friends array is exactly what we need because the posts in our social network are linked to the users' profiles by their IDs.

The next step is to establish a connection to the database and query only those records that match the specific IDs, as follows:

```
case 'GET':
  getCurrentUser(function(user) {
    if(!user.friends) {
      user.friends = [];
    }
    getDatabaseConnection(function(db) {
      var collection = db.collection('content');
      collection.find({
        $query: {
          userId: { $in: [user._id.toString()].concat(user.friends) }
        },
        $orderby: {
          date: -1
        }
      }).toArray(function(err, result) {
        result.forEach(function(value, index, arr) {
          arr[index].id = ObjectId(value.id);
          delete arr[index].userId;
        });
        response({
          posts: result
        }, res);
      });
    });
  }, req, res);
  break;
```

We are going to read the records from the content collection. The find method accepts an object that has the $query and $orderby properties. In the first one, we will put our criteria. In this particular case, we want to get all the records' IDs that are a part of the friends array. In order to create such a query, we need the $in operator. It accepts an array. Along with the posts of the user's friends, we need to show the posts of the user. So, we will create an array with an item — the ID of the current user — and concatenate it with friends, as follows:

```
[user._id.toString()].concat(user.friends)
```

After a successful query, the userId property is deleted because it is not needed. In the content collection, we keep the text of the message and the name of the owner. In the end, the records are sent attached to the posts property.

With the additions made in the preceding code, our backend returns the posts made by the current user and their friends. All we have to do is update the controller of our home page and use the API's method. Right after the code listening for the post event, we add the following code:

```
var getPosts = function() {
  model.fetch(function(err, result) {
    if(!err) {
      self.set('posts', result.posts);
    }
  });
};
getPosts();
```

The calling of the fetch method triggers the GET request to the API at the model's endpoint — /api/content. The process is wrapped in a function because the same action will happen when a new post is created. As we already know, if model.create succeeds, a callback is fired. We will add getPosts() there so that the user sees his/her newest post in the feed:

```
// frontend/js/controllers/Home.js
model.create(formData, function(error, result) {
  self.set('text', '');
  if(error) {
    self.set('error', error.error);
  } else {
    self.set('error', false);
```

```
            self.set('success', 'The post is saved
            successfully.<br />What about adding another one?');
            getPosts();
        }
    });
```

What the `getPosts` function produces as a result are lists of objects stored in a local variable called `posts`. The same variable is accessible in the Ractive.js template. We need to loop through the items in the array and display the information on the screen, as follows:

```
// frontend/tpl/home.html
<header>
  <navigation></navigation>
</header>
<div class="hero">
  {{#if posting === true}}
    <form enctype="multipart/form-data" method="post">
      ...
    </form>
    {{#each posts:index}}
      <div class="content-item">
        <h2>{{posts[index].userName}}</h2>
        {{posts[index].text}}
      </div>
    {{/each}}
  {{else}}
    <h1>Node.js by example</h1>
  {{/if}}
</div>
<appfooter />
```

Just after the form, we use the `each` operator to show the author and the text of the post.

At this point, the users in our network will be able to create and browse messages in the form of text blocks. In the next section, we will extend the functionalities that we have written so far and make the uploading of images along with the text possible.

Posting files

We are building a single-page application. One of the characteristics of such applications is that all the operations happen without a page reload. Uploading files without changing the page was always tricky. In the past, we used solutions that involved hidden iframes or small Flash applications. Thankfully, when HTML5 arrived, it introduced the **FormData** interface.

The popular Ajax is possible because of the `XMLHttpRequest` object. Back in 2005, Jesse James Garrett coined the term "Ajax", and we started using it to make HTTP requests within JavaScript. It became easy to perform the GET or POST requests in the following way:

```
var http = new XMLHttpRequest();
var url = "/api/content";
var params = "text=message&author=name";
http.open("POST", url, true);

http.setRequestHeader("Content-type", "application/x-www-form-
urlencoded");
http.setRequestHeader("Content-length", params.length);
http.setRequestHeader("Connection", "close");

http.onreadystatechange = function() {
  if(http.readyState == 4 && http.status === 200) {
    alert(http.responseText);
  }
}

http.send(params);
```

The preceding code generates a proper POST requests and even sets the right headers. The problem is that the parameters are represented as a string. The forming of such strings requires additional effort. It is also difficult to send files. It can be quite challenging.

The FormData interface solves this problem. We create an object that is a set of key/value pairs representing form fields and their values. Then, we pass this object to the `send` method of the `XMLHTTPRequest` class:

```
var formData = new FormData();
var fileInput = document.querySelector('input[type="file"]');
var url = '/api/content';
```

```
formData.append("username", "John Black");
formData.append("id", 123456);
formData.append("userfile", fileInput.files[0]);

var request = new XMLHttpRequest();
request.open("POST", url);
request.send(formData);
```

All we have to do is use the `append` method and specify the `input` DOM element with the `file` type. The rest is done by the browser.

To provide the ability to upload files, we need to add the UI element for file selection. Here is how the form in `home.html` template looks:

```
<form enctype="multipart/form-data" method="post">
  <h3>What is on your mind?</h3>
  {{#if error && error != ''}}
    <div class="error">{{error}}</div>
  {{/if}}
  {{#if success && success != ''}}
    <div class="success">{{{success}}}</div>
  {{/if}}
  <label for="text">Text</label>
  <textarea value="{{text}}"></textarea>
  <input type="file" name="file" />
  <input type="button" value="Post" on-click="post" />
</form>
```

The same code but with a new `input` element with type equal to `file`. So far, the implementation in our controller that sends the `POST` requests doesn't use the FormData interface. Let's change this and update the `controllers/Home.js` file:

```
this.on('post', function() {
  var files = this.find('input[type="file"]').files;
  var formData = new FormData();
  if(files.length > 0) {
    var file = files[0];
    if(file.type.match('image.*')) {
      formData.append('files', file, file.name);
    }
  }
}
```

```
      formData.append('text', this.get('text'));
      model.create(formData, function(error, result) {
        self.set('text', '');
        if(error) {
          self.set('error', error.error);
        } else {
          self.set('error', false);
          self.set('success', 'The post is saved
          successfully.<br />What about adding another one?');
          getPosts();
        }
      });
    });
```

The code is changed. So, the code creates a new `FormData` object and uses the `append` method for collecting the information needed for the new post. We make sure that the files selected by the user are appended. By default, the HTML input provides a selection of only one file. However, we can add the `multiple` attribute and the browser will allow us to choose more than one file. It is worth mentioning that we filter the selected files and only use the images.

After the latest changes, the `create` method of our model accepts the `FormData` object and not a plain JavaScript object. So, we have to update the model, too:

```
// models/Content.js
create: function(formData, callback) {
  var self = this;
  ajax.request({
    url: this.get('url'),
    method: 'POST',
    formData: formData,
    json: true
  })
  .done(function(result) {
    callback(null, result);
  })
  .fail(function(xhr) {
    callback(JSON.parse(xhr.responseText));
  });
}
```

The `data` property is replaced with the `formData` one. Now we know that the frontend sends the selected files to the API. However, we do not have the code that handles the `multipart/form-data` type of the `POST` data. The processing of files sent through the `POST` request is not that simple, and `processPOSTRequest` will not do the job in this case.

Node.js has a big community, and there are thousands of modules available. The `formidable` module is what we are going to use. It has a fairly simple API and it handles requests containing files. What happens during the file upload is that `formidable` saves the file in a specific location on the server's hard disk. Then, we receive the path to the resource. Finally, we have to decide what to do with it.

In the `backend/API.js` file, the application flow is split into the `GET` and `POST` requests. We are going to update a major part of the `POST` case. The following lines contain the `formidable` initialization:

```
case 'POST':
  var formidable = require('formidable');
  var uploadDir = __dirname + '/../static/uploads/';
  var form = new formidable.IncomingForm();
  form.multiples = true;
  form.parse(req, function(err, data, files) {
    // ...
  });
break;
```

As we mentioned before, the module saves the uploaded files in a temporary folder on the hard drive. The `uploadDir` variable contains a more appropriate place for the users' images. The callback passed to the `parse` function of `formidable` receives the normal text fields in the `data` argument and uploads the images in `files`.

In order to avoid the long chain of nested JavaScript callbacks, we will extract some logic into the function definitions. For example, the moving of files from the `temporary` to the `static` folder can be performed in the following way:

```
var processFiles = function(userId, callback) {
  if(files.files) {
    var fileName = userId + '_' + files.files.name;
    var filePath = uploadDir + fileName;
    fs.rename(files.files.path, filePath, function() {
      callback(fileName);
    });
```

```
    } else {
      callback();
    }
  };
```

We don't want to mix the files of different users. So, we will use the ID of the user and create his/her own folder. There are a few other issues that we may have to take care of. For example, we can create subfolders for every file so that we can prevent the overwriting of the resources that are already uploaded. However, to keep the code as simple as possible, we will stop here.

Here is the complete code that saves the post to the database:

```
case 'POST':
  var uploadDir = __dirname + '/../static/uploads/';
  var formidable = require('formidable');
  var form = new formidable.IncomingForm();
  form.multiples = true;
  form.parse(req, function(err, data, files) {
    if(!data.text || data.text === '') {
      error('Please add some text.', res);
    } else {
      var processFiles = function(userId, callback) {
        if(files.files) {
          var fileName = userId + '_' + files.files.name;
          var filePath = uploadDir + fileName;
          fs.rename(files.files.path, filePath, function(err) {
            if(err) throw err;
            callback(fileName);
          });
        } else {
          callback();
        }
      };
      var done = function() {
        response({
          success: 'OK'
        }, res);
      }
```

```
getDatabaseConnection(function(db) {
    getCurrentUser(function(user) {
        var collection = db.collection('content');
        data.userId = user._id.toString();
        data.userName = user.firstName + ' ' + user.lastName;
        data.date = new Date();
        processFiles(user._id, function(file) {
            if(file) {
                data.file = file;
            }
            collection.insert(data, done);
        });
    }, req, res);
    });
    }
});
break;
```

We still need a connection to the database and the fetching of the current user's profile. The difference here is that we attach a new `file` property to the object stored in MongoDB.

In the end, we have to update the template of the home page so that it shows the uploaded file:

```
{{#each posts:index}}
    <div class="content-item">
        <h2>{{posts[index].userName}}</h2>
        {{posts[index].text}}
        {{#if posts[index].file}}
        <img src="/static/uploads/{{posts[index].file}}" />
        {{/if}}
    </div>
{{/each}}
```

Now, the `each` loop checks whether there is a file that comes with the text of the post. If yes, it displays an `img` tag that shows the image. With this last addition, the users of our social network will be able to create content that consists of text and pictures.

Summary

In this chapter, we did something that is very important for our application. We implemented content creation and delivery by extending our backend API. A couple of changes were made to the frontend too.

In the next chapter, we will continue adding new features. We will make the creating of branded pages and events possible.

8
Creating Pages and Events

Chapter 7, Posting Content, covered the posting of content. We gave an interface to user to send text and images to our database. Later, these resources were shown as a message feed on the home page. In this chapter, we will learn how to create pages and events that are attached to these pages. Here is the plan that we are going to follow:

- Refactoring the API
- Adding a form to create pages
- Creating a record in the database
- Showing the currently added pages
- Showing a specific page
- Posting a comment to a page
- Showing comments
- Managing events attached to a particular page

Refactoring the API

If you check the files that you ended up with in the previous chapter, you will see that the `backend/API.js` file is quite big. It will get more and more difficult to work with. We are going to refactor this part of our system.

We have a bunch of helper methods that are used all over the route handlers. Functions such as `response`, `error`, and `getDatabaseConnection` may be placed in an external module. We will create a new `api` folder under the `backend` directory. The newly created `helpers.js` file will host all these utility functions:

```
// backend/api/helpers.js
var MongoClient = require('mongodb').MongoClient;
```

```
var querystring = require('querystring');
var database;

var response = function(result, res) { ... };
var error = function(message, res) { ... };
var getDatabaseConnection = function(callback) { ... };
var processPOSTRequest = function(req, callback) { ... };
var validEmail = function(value) { ... };
var getCurrentUser = function(callback, req, res) { ... };

module.exports = {
  response: response,
  error: error,
  getDatabaseConnection: getDatabaseConnection,
  processPOSTRequest: processPOSTRequest,
  validEmail: validEmail,
  getCurrentUser: getCurrentUser
};
```

We will skip the implementation of the functions so that we don't bloat the chapter with the code that we already saw. We also copied a few variables used by the methods.

The next step of our refactoring is the extraction of all the route handlers into their own methods. So far, the file is structured as follows:

```
var Router = require('../frontend/js/lib/router')();
Router
.add('api/version', function(req, res) { ... })
.add('api/user/login', function(req, res) { ... })
```

The whole structure is a bunch of route definitions and their respective handlers. We often have a `switch` statement that checks the type of the request. In practice, every function (`req`, `res`) can be represented by an independent module. Again, we are not going to paste the content of all the created files, but we will talk about the final result. After the refactoring, we will have the following structure:

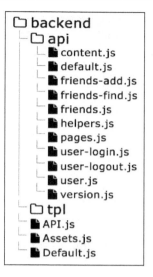

The number of lines in API.js decreased significantly. Now, we have just the route's definition and its handlers:

```
var Router = require('../frontend/js/lib/router')();
Router
.add('api/version', require('./api/version'))
.add('api/user/login', require('./api/user-login'))
.add('api/user/logout', require('./api/user-logout'))
.add('api/user', require('./api/user'))
.add('api/friends/find', require('./api/friends-find'))
.add('api/friends/add', require('./api/friends-add'))
.add('api/friends', require('./api/friends'))
.add('api/content', require('./api/content'))
.add('api/pages/:id', require('./api/pages'))
.add('api/pages', require('./api/pages'))
.add(require('./api/default'));
module.exports = function(req, res) {
  Router.check(req.url, [req, res]);
}
```

The functions that the new files export are still the same. The only thing that you should consider is the helper functions. You have to provide them in all the new modules. For example, the `friends.js` file contains the following:

```
var ObjectId = require('mongodb').ObjectID;
var helpers = require('./helpers');
var response = helpers.response;
var error = helpers.error;
var getDatabaseConnection = helpers.getDatabaseConnection;
var getCurrentUser = helpers.getCurrentUser;

module.exports = function(req, res) {
    ...
}
```

Check out the files that came with this chapter for the complete source code.

Adding a form to create pages

Every user in our social network should be able to browse and create pages. This is a completely new functionality. So, we will need a new route and controller.

1. Let's start by updating `frontend/js/app.js`, as follows:

```
.add('pages', function() {
  if(userModel.isLogged()) {
    var p = new Pages();
    showPage(p);
  } else {
    Router.navigate('login');
  }
})
.add(function() {
  Router.navigate('home');
})
```

2. Just above the default handler, we will register a route that creates an instance of a new controller called `Pages`. We will make sure that the visitor is logged in before seeing the page. In the same file, at the top, we will add `var Pages = require('./controllers/Pages');`.

3. Let's dive into the `controllers/Page.js` file and see how you can bootstrap the controller:

```
module.exports = Ractive.extend({
  template: require('../../tpl/pages'),
  components: {
    navigation: require('../views/Navigation'),
    appfooter: require('../views/Footer')
  },
  data: { },
  onrender: function() { }
});
```

4. The `onrender` function is still empty, but we will fill it in the next few sections. The template that stands behind this page is located in `frontend/tpl/pages.html`:

```
<header>
  <navigation></navigation>
</header>
<div class="hero">
  <form enctype="multipart/form-data" method="post">
    <h3>Add a new page</h3>
    {{#if error && error != ''}}
      <div class="error">{{error}}</div>
    {{/if}}
    {{#if success && success != ''}}
      <div class="success">{{{success}}}</div>
    {{/if}}
    <label>Title</label>
    <textarea value="{{title}}"></textarea>
    <label>Description</label>
    <textarea value="{{description}}"></textarea>
    <input type="button" value="Create" on-click="create" />
  </form>
</div>
<appfooter />
```

The code looks similar to the one used in the previous chapter when we created the UI to add content. We have placeholders for successful and error messages. There are two variables, `title` and `description`, and a button dispatching the `create` event.

Creating a record in the database

Let's continue and handle the situation where the user presses the **Create** button.
After the user performs this action, we have to get the content of the text areas and
submit a request to the backend. So, we need a new model. Let's call it `Pages.js` and
save it under the `models` directory:

```
// frontend/js/models/Pages.js
var ajax = require('../lib/Ajax');
var Base = require('./Base');
module.exports = Base.extend({
  data: {
    url: '/api/pages'
  },
  create: function(formData, callback) {
    var self = this;
    ajax.request({
      url: this.get('url'),
      method: 'POST',
      formData: formData,
      json: true
    })
    .done(function(result) {
      callback(null, result);
    })
    .fail(function(xhr) {
      callback(JSON.parse(xhr.responseText));
    });
  }
});
```

We already talked about the `FormData` interface in the previous chapter. The API
endpoint that we are going to use is `/api/pages`. This is the URL where we will
send a `POST` request.

Now that we have the form displayed and the model ready for backend
communication, we can continue with the code in our controller.
The `onrender` handler is the right place to listen to the `create` event:

```
onrender: function() {
  var model = new PagesModel();
  var self = this;
  this.on('create', function() {
    var formData = new FormData();
    formData.append('title', this.get('title'));
```

```
      formData.append('description', this.get('description'));
      model.create(formData, function(error, result) {
        if(error) {
          self.set('error', error.error);
        } else {
          self.set('title', '');
          self.set('description', '');
          self.set('error', false);
          self.set('success', 'The page was created successfully.
        }
      });
    });
  }
```

The initialization of the model is at the top. After fetching the data filled by the user, we will call the `create` method of the model and handle the response afterwards. If something goes wrong, our application displays an error message.

The last step in this section is updating the API so that we can keep the data in our database. There is still no route that matches `/api/pages`. So, let's add one:

```
// backend/API.js
.add('api/pages', require('./api/pages'))
.add(require('./api/default'));
```

We refactored the API so that the code that will process the requests goes to the new `/backend/api/pages.js` file. In the first few lines, there are shortcuts to our helper methods:

```
var ObjectId = require('mongodb').ObjectID;
var helpers = require('./helpers');
var response = helpers.response;
var error = helpers.error;
var getDatabaseConnection = helpers.getDatabaseConnection;
var getCurrentUser = helpers.getCurrentUser;
```

Here is the code that creates a new record in a new `pages` collection. It may look a little long, but a major part of the same is already covered in *Chapter 7, Posting Content*:

```
module.exports = function(req, res) {
  var user;
  if(req.session && req.session.user) {
    user = req.session.user;
  } else {
    error('You must be logged in in order to use this
method.', res);
```

```
        return;
    }
switch(req.method) {
    case 'GET': break;
    case 'POST':
        var formidable = require('formidable');
        var form = new formidable.IncomingForm();
        form.parse(req, function(err, formData, files) {
            var data = {
                title: formData.title,
                description: formData.description
            };
            if(!data.title || data.title === '') {
                error('Please add some title.', res);
            } else if(!data.description || data.description === '') {
                error('Please add some description.', res);
            } else {
                var done = function() {
                    response({
                        success: 'OK'
                    }, res);
                }
                getDatabaseConnection(function(db) {
                    getCurrentUser(function(user) {
                        var collection = db.collection('pages');
                        data.userId = user._id.toString();
                        data.userName = user.firstName + ' ' + user.lastName;
                        data.date = new Date();
                        collection.insert(data, done);
                    }, req, res);
                });
            }
        });
    break;
    };
}
```

The creating and browsing of pages is a feature reserved only for the logged in users.
The first few lines of the exported function check whether the current visitor has
a valid session. The frontend sends a POST request without a file, but we will still
require the formidable module because it has a nice programming interface and
is easy to use. Every page should have a title and a description, and we will check
whether they exist. If everything is okay, we will create a new record in the database
by using the well-known getDatabaseConnection function.

Showing the currently added pages

It is nice that we started keeping the created pages in the database. However, it will also be great to show the pages to the users so that they can visit them and add comments. In order to do that, we have to modify our API so that it returns the page information. If you look at the preceding code, you will see that there is a GET case that was left empty. The following codes gets all the pages, sorts them by date, and sends them to the browser:

```
case 'GET':
  getDatabaseConnection(function(db) {
    var collection = db.collection('pages');
    collection.find({
      $query: { },
      $orderby: {
        date: -1
      }
    }).toArray(function(err, result) {
      result.forEach(function(value, index, arr) {
        arr[index].id = value._id;
        delete arr[index].userId;
      });
      response({
        pages: result
      }, res);
    });
  });
break;
```

Before sending the JSON object to the frontend, we will delete the ID of the creator. The name of the user is already there and it is a good practice to keep these IDs only in the backend.

After a quick restart, the Node.js server returns the created pages when we visit /api/pages. Let's move forward and update the controllers/Pages.js file in the client side of our app. In the onrender handler, we will append the following code:

```
var getPages = function() {
  model.fetch(function(err, result) {
    if(!err) {
      self.set('pages', result.pages);
    } else {
      self.set('error', err.error);
    }
  });
};
getPages();
```

We will wrap the newly added logic in a function because we have to go through the same things when a new page is created. The model does most of the job. We will simply assign an array of objects to a `pages` variable. This variable is used in the template of the component — `frontend/tpl/pages.html` — as follows:

```
{{#each pages:index}}
  <div class="content-item">
    <h2>{{pages[index].title}}</h2>
    <p><small>Created by {{pages[index].userName}}</small></p>
    <p>{{pages[index].description}}</p>
    <p><a href="/pages/{{pages[index].id}}" class="button">Visit the
        page</a></p>
  </div>
{{/each}}
```

In the next section, you will learn how to show only a particular page. The link that we added in this code forwards the user to a new address. This link is a URL that contains the information for only one page.

Showing a specific page

Again, to show a specific page, we need to update our API. We have the code that returns all the pages, but there is no solution if you want to return only one of the pages. We will use the ID of the page for sure. So, here is a new route that can be added to `backend/API.js`:

```
.add('api/pages/:id', require('./api/pages'))
.add('api/pages', require('./api/pages'))
```

You should keep in mind that the order of the routes is important. The one that contains the ID of the page should be above the one that shows the list of the pages. Otherwise, the application will proceed with listing a new URL all the time, but we will keep the same handler. If there are any dynamic parts in the address, our router sends an additional parameter to the function. So in `backend/api/pages.js`, we will change `module.exports = function(req, res)` to `module.exports = function(req, res, params)`. In the same file, we will fetch all the pages from the database. In this case, we want the code to be modified so that the function returns only one record that matches the ID that was passed in the URL. So far, our MongoDB query looks like this:

```
collection.find({
  $query: { },
  $orderby: {
    date: -1
  }
}
```

In practice, we have no criteria. Now, let's change the preceding code to the following:

```
var query;
if(params && params.id) {
  query = { _id: ObjectId(params.id) };
} else {
  query = {};
}
collection.find({
  $query: query,
  $orderby: {
    date: -1
  }
}
```

By defining a `query` variable, we make the response of this API method conditional. It depends on the existence of the ID in the URL. If there is any such ID, it still returns an array of objects, but there is only one item inside.

In the frontend, we can use the same approach, or in other words, the same controller that covers both the cases—showing all the pages and showing only one page. We register a new route handler that forwards the user to the same `Pages` controller, as follows:

```
// frontend/js/app.js
.add('pages/:id', function(params) {
  if(userModel.isLogged()) {
    var p = new Pages({
      data: {
        pageId: params.id
      }
    });
    showPage(p);
  } else {
    Router.navigate('login');
  }
})
```

This time, we passed the configuration during the initialization of the controller. The setting of values in the data property creates variables that are later available inside the component and its template. In our case, pageId will be accessible via this.get('pageId'). If the variable does not exist, then we are in the mode that shows all the pages. The following lines display the title and the description of a single page:

```
// controllers/Page.js
onrender: function() {
  var model = new PagesModel();
  var self = this;

  var pageId = this.get('pageId');
  if(pageId) {
    model.getPage(pageId, function(err, result) {
      if(!err && result.pages.length > 0) {
        var page = result.pages[0];
        self.set('pageTitle', page.title);
        self.set('pageDescription', page.description);
      } else {
        self.set('pageTitle', 'Missing page.');
      }
    });
    return;
  }

  ...
```

The model that we used so far performs the POST and GET requests, but we can't use them in this case. They are reserved for other functionalities. We need another method that accepts the ID of the page. This is why we will add a new getPage function:

```
// models/Pages.js
getPage: function(pageId, callback) {
  var self = this;
  ajax.request({
    url: this.get('url') + '/' + pageId,
    method: 'GET',
    json: true
  })
  .done(function(result) {
    callback(null, result);
  })
  .fail(function(xhr) {
    callback(JSON.parse(xhr.responseText));
  });
}
```

We do not have any data to send. We have only a different endpoint URL. The ID of the page is appended at the end of the /api/pages string. This section started with changes in the backend so that we know that the API returns an array of one element. The rest is setting pageTitle and pageDescription.

In the template, we use the same pattern. You can check whether pageId exists and this will be enough to find out whether we have to show one or many pages:

```
{{#if pageId}}
  <div class="hero">
    <h1>{{pageTitle}}</h1>
    <p>{{pageDescription}}</p>
  </div>
  <hr />
{{else}}
  <div class="hero">
    <form enctype="multipart/form-data" method="post">
      . . .
    </form>
  </div>
  {{#each pages:index}}
    . . .
  {{/each}}
{{/if}}
```

After changing frontend/tpl/pages.html, we have a unique URL for every page. However, a page displayed with a static title and description is not very interesting for the users. Let's add a comments section.

Posting a comment to a page

Before reaching the part where we send and process an HTTP request, we have to provide a user interface to create a comment. We will add a form just below the title and description of the page in frontend/tpl/pages.html:

```
<form enctype="multipart/form-data" method="post">
  <h3>Add a comment for this page</h3>
  {{#if error && error != ''}}
    <div class="error">{{error}}</div>
  {{/if}}
  {{#if success && success != ''}}
    <div class="success">{{{success}}}</div>
```

```
   {{/if}}
   <label for="text">Text</label>
   <textarea value="{{text}}"></textarea>
   <input type="button" value="Post" on-click="add-comment" />
</form>
```

The event that is dispatched after clicking on the button is `add-comment`. The `Pages` controller should handle it and fire a request to the backend.

If you stop and think a bit about how the comments look, you will notice that they are similar to the regular user posts that are visible in the user's feed. So, instead of creating a new collection or storing complex data structures in the `pages` collection, we will save our comments as regular posts. For the code on the client side, this means one more use case of the `ContentModel` class:

```
// controllers/Pages.js
this.on('add-comment', function() {
  var contentModel = new ContentModel();
  var formData = new FormData();
  formData.append('text', this.get('text'));
  formData.append('pageId', pageId);
  contentModel.create(formData, function(error, result) {
    self.set('text', '');
    if(error) {
      self.set('error', error.error);
    } else {
      self.set('error', false);
      self.set('success', 'The post is saved successfully.');
    }
  });
});
```

The usage of the model is the same except for one thing — we send an additional `pageId` variable. We need something to distinguish the posts made in the home page and those made as comments. The API will still not save `pageId`. So, we have to make a little update in `backend/api/content.js`, as follows:

```
form.parse(req, function(err, formData, files) {
  var data = {
    text: formData.text
  };
  if(formData.pageId) {
    data.pageId = formData.pageId;
  }
  ...
```

When the user is making a comment, the record in the database will contain the pageId property. This is enough to keep the comments away from the home page. Also, from another point of view, it is enough to display only the comments for a particular page.

Showing the comments

We should update the API method that returns the pages as objects. Along with the title and description, we have to present a new comments property. Let's open backend/api/pages.js and create a function to fetch comments:

```
var getComments = function(pageId, callback) {
  var collection = db.collection('content');
  collection.find({
    $query: {
      pageId: pageId
    },
    $orderby: {
      date: -1
    }
  }).toArray(function(err, result) {
    result.forEach(function(value, index, arr) {
      delete arr[index].userId;
      delete arr[index]._id;
    });
    callback(result);
  });
}
```

The key moment in the preceding method is the forming of the MongoDB query. This is the place where we filter the posts and fetch only those that are made for the page that matches the passed ID. The following is the updated code corresponding to the GET request:

```
getDatabaseConnection(function(db) {
  var query;
  if(params && params.id) {
    query = { _id: ObjectId(params.id) };
  } else {
    query = {};
  }
  var collection = db.collection('pages');
  var getComments = function(pageId, callback) { ... }
  collection.find({
```

```
        $query: query,
        $orderby: {
          date: -1
        }
    }).toArray(function(err, result) {
      result.forEach(function(value, index, arr) {
        arr[index].id = value._id;
        delete arr[index]._id;
        delete arr[index].userId;
      });
      if(params.id && result.length > 0) {
        getComments(params.id, function(comments) {
          result[0].comments = comments;
          response({
            pages: result
          }, res);
        });
      } else {
        response({
          pages: result
        }, res);
      }
    });
  });
```

There are two types of responses. The first one is used when we have an ID added to the URL or, in other words, when we show information about a page. In this case, we have to also fetch the comments. In the other case, we do not need the comments because we will be displaying only the list. Checking whether `params.id` exists is enough to decide which type of response to send.

Once the backend starts returning the comments, we will write the code that shows them in the browser. In `frontend/js/controllers/Pages.js`, we will set the title and description of the page. We can directly pass the `comments` array to the template and loop over the post, as follows:

```
var showPage = function() {
  model.getPage(pageId, function(err, result) {
    if(!err && result.pages.length > 0) {
      var page = result.pages[0];
      self.set('pageTitle', page.title);
      self.set('pageDescription', page.description);
      self.set('comments', page.comments);
    } else {
      self.set('pageTitle', 'Missing page.');
    }
  });
}
showPage();
```

We wrapped the calling of `model.getPage` in a function so that we can fire it again once a new comment is added.

Here is a small update in the template needed to display the posts below the form:

```
{{#each comments:index}}
  <div class="content-item">
    <h2>{{comments[index].userName}}</h2>
    <p>{{comments[index].text}}</p>
  </div>
{{/each}}
```

Managing events attached to a particular page

The last feature that we will add in this chapter is the events attached to some of the created pages. So far, we have comments that are actually normal posts kept in the `content` collection. We will extend the implementation and create another type of post. These posts will still have a `pageId` property so that they are different from the feed's posts. However, we will introduce an `eventDate` variable.

In the frontend, we need a new URL. We should keep the same pattern that contains the ID of the page. This is important because we want to display the events in the right place and we don't want to mix them with the list of the pages. Here is the new route registration:

```
// frontend/js/app.js
.add('pages/:id/:events', function(params) {
  if(userModel.isLogged()) {
    var p = new Pages({
      data: {
        pageId: params.id,
        showEvents: true
      }
    });
    showPage(p);
  } else {
    Router.navigate('login');
  }
})
```

The template of the `Pages` controller should surely be changed. We need to support two views. The first one shows a form and comments, and the second one shows a form and a list of events. The `showEvents` variable will tell us which variant to render:

```
// frontend/tpl/pages.html
{{#if showEvents}}
  <form enctype="multipart/form-data" method="post">
    <a href="/pages/{{pageId}}" class="button m-right right">View
      comments</a>
    <h3>Add new event</h3>
    ...
  </form>
  {{#each events:index}} … {{/each}}
{{else}}
  <form enctype="multipart/form-data" method="post">
    <a href="/pages/{{pageId}}/events" class="button right">View
      events</a>
    <h3>Add a comment for this page</h3>
    ...
  </form>
  {{#each comments:index}} … {{/each}}
{{/if}}
```

In order to switch between the views, we added two additional links. While we are checking the comments, we will see **View events**, and when we jump to the events, we will see **View comments**.

The `controllers/Pages.js` file needs a solid update, too. Most importantly, we need to add a handler of the `add-event` event that comes from the template. It is fired when the user presses the button in the new event form. It looks like this:

```
this.on('add-event', function() {
  var contentModel = new ContentModel();
  var formData = new FormData();
  formData.append('text', this.get('text'));
  formData.append('eventDate', this.get('date'));
  formData.append('pageId', pageId);
  contentModel.create(formData, function(error, result) {
    ...
  });
});
```

It is similar to adding a comment, but for the additional `eventDate` property. It should also be set as a property of the object that goes to the `content` collection:

```
// backend/api/content.js
if(formData.pageId) {
  data.pageId = formData.pageId;
}
if(formData.eventDate) {
  data.eventDate = formData.eventDate;
}
```

Another change in the same frontend controller is with regard to showing the list of events (posts) in the template. When we get the title and description of the page, we know that we will receive a `comments` property. The backend will be updated in a minute, but we will assume that we will also have an `events` property. So, we will simply send the array to the template:

```
self.set('events', page.events);
```

In the backend, we have already fetched the records from the `content` collection that belongs to the current page. The problem is that the records are now a mixture of comments and events. The `getComments` function that we added in the previous section can be changed to `getPageItems`, and the implementation of it basically looks like this:

```
var getPageItems = function(pageId, callback) {
  var collection = db.collection('content');
  collection.find({
    $query: {
      pageId: pageId
    },
    $orderby: {
      date: -1
    }
  }).toArray(function(err, result) {
    var comments = [];
    var events = [];
    result.forEach(function(value, index, arr) {
      delete value.userId;
      delete value._id;
      if(value.eventDate) {
        events.push(value);
      } else {
        comments.push(value);
      }
```

```
    });
    events.sort(function(a, b) {
      return a.eventDate > b.eventDate;
    });
    callback(comments, events);
  });
}
```

We formed the two different `events` and `comments` arrays. Based on the existence of `eventDate`, we will fill them with records. Just before executing the callback, we will sort the events by date, showing the earlier event first. The last thing that we will do is use `getPageItem`:

```
getPageItems(params.id, function(comments, events) {
  result[0].comments = comments;
  result[0].events = events;
  ...
}
```

Summary

In this chapter, we extended our social network. Every customer is now able to create their own pages and leave comments there or create events related to the page. A bunch of new components were added to our architecture. We successfully reused the code from the previous chapters, which is good if we want to keep our codebase small.

In *Chapter 9, Tagging, Sharing, and Liking*, we will discuss the tagging, liking, and sharing of posts.

Tagging, Sharing, and Liking

Chapter 8, Creating Pages and Events, was about creating pages and attaching events to them. We also made the posting of comments possible. In this part of the book, we will add three new features. Almost every social network contains some way to like a post. It is a nice way to rank the posts that you are interested in. Sharing is another popular process that comprises of posting an already existing post. Sometimes, we want to refer a post to some of our friends. In these cases, we **tag** people. These three functionalities will be implemented in this chapter. Here are the sections that will guide us through the development process:

- Selecting friends and sending their IDs to the backend
- Storing the tagged users and displaying them in the user's feed
- Sharing a post
- Liking posts and counting the number of likes
- Showing the number of likes

Selecting friends and sending their IDs to the backend

We will start with the tagging of not only random users but also the friends of the current user. The functionality that we want to build will be placed on the home page. The form that creates a new post will contain a list of checkboxes. The very first step will be to fetch the friends from the API. In *Chapter 6, Adding Friendship Capabilities,* we already did that. We have a models/Friends.js file that queries the Node.js server and returns a list of users. So, let's use it. At the top of controllers/ Home.js, we will add the following:

```
var Friends = require('../models/Friends');
```

Later, in the `onrender` handler, we will use the required module. The result of the API will be set as a value to a local `friends` variable in the following way:

```
var friends = new Friends();
friends.fetch(function(err, result) {
  if (err) { throw err; }
  self.set('friends', result.friends);
});
```

The controller has the user's friends in its data structure, and we may update the template. We will make a loop through the records and display a checkbox for every user in the following way:

```
// frontend/tpl/home.html
{{#if friends.length > 0}}
<p>Tag friends:
{{#each friends:index}}
  <label>
    <input type="checkbox" name="{{taggedFriends}}"
      value="{{friends[index].id}}" />
    {{friends[index].firstName}}
    {{friends[index].lastName}}
  </label>
{{/each}}
</p>
{{/if}}
```

The Ractive.js framework nicely handles groups of checkboxes. In our case, the JavaScript component will receive a variable called `taggedFriends`. It will be an array of the selected users or an empty array if the user does not tick anything. The expected output is a list of the user's friends in the form of checkboxes and labels.

Once Gulp compiles the new version of the template and we hit the refresh button of the browser, we will see our friends on the screen. We will select some of them, fill the content of the post, and press the **Post** button. The application sends a request to the API but without the tagged friends. One more change is needed to fix that. In the `controllers/Home.js` file, we have to use the value of the `taggedFriends` variable, as follows:

```
formData.append('text', this.get('text'));
formData.append('taggedFriends', JSON.stringify(this.
get('taggedFriends')));
model.create(formData, function(error, result) {
  ...
});
```

The FormData API accepts only Blob, file, or string values. We cannot send an array of strings. So, we will serialize `taggedFriends` to a string using `JSON.stringify`. In the next section, we will use `JSON.parse` to convert the string to an object. The `JSON` interface is available in both the browser and Node.js environments.

Storing the tagged users and displaying them in the user's feed

Along with the text and files, we now send a list of user IDs—users that should be tagged in the post. As mentioned before, they come to the server in the form of a string. We need to use `JSON.parse` to convert them into a regular array. The following lines are part of the `backend/api/content.js` module:

```
var form = new formidable.IncomingForm();
form.multiples = true;
form.parse(req, function(err, formData, files) {
  var data = {
    text: formData.text
  };
  if(formData.pageId) {
    data.pageId = formData.pageId;
  }
  if(formData.eventDate) {
    data.eventDate = formData.eventDate;
  }
  if(formData.taggedFriends) {
    data.taggedFriends = JSON.parse(formData.taggedFriends);
  }
  ...
```

The `content.js` module is the place where `formidable` provides the data sent by the frontend. At the end of this code snippet, we reconstructed the array from the previously serialized string.

We can easily go with only that change and store the `data` object. Indeed, in the client side, we will receive the post containing the `taggedFriends` property. However, we are interested in showing the names of the friends and not their IDs. If the frontend controller has IDs and needs names, then it should perform another HTTP request to the API. This will probably lead to a large number of API queries, especially if we have many messages displayed. To prevent such a situation, we will fetch the names of the tagged people during the fetching of the post in the backend. This approach has its own disadvantages, but it is still better compared to the variant mentioned earlier.

Let's create a function that wraps the needed logic and use it before saving the information in the database:

```
// backend/api/content.js
var getFriendsProfiles = function(db, ids, callback) {
  if(ids && ids.length > 0) {
    var collection = db.collection('users');
    ids.forEach(function(value, index, arr) {
      arr[index] = ObjectId(value);
    });
    collection.find({
      _id: { $in: ids }
    }).toArray(function(err, friends) {
      var result = [];
      friends.forEach(function(friend) {
        result.push(friend.firstName + ' ' + friend.lastName);
      });
      callback(result);
    });
  } else {
    callback([]);
  }
}
```

We prepared the IDs of the users for the MongoDB query. In this case, the $in operator is needed because we want to fetch the records of the IDs that match any of the items in the ids array. When the MongoDB driver returns the data, we create another array that contains the names of the friends. GetFriendsProfiles will be used in the next few pages, where we will update the posts' feed fetching.

The actual storing of the data is still the same. The only difference is that the data object now contains the taggedFriends property:

```
getDatabaseConnection(function(db) {
  getCurrentUser(function(user) {
    var collection = db.collection('content');
    data.userId = user._id.toString();
    data.userName = user.firstName + ' ' + user.lastName;
    data.date = new Date();
    processFiles(user._id, function(file) {
      if(file) {
        data.file = file;
      }
      collection.insert(data, done);
    });
  }, req, res);
});
```

If we create a new post and check the record in the database, we will see something like this:

```
{
   "text": "What a nice day. Isn't it?",
   "taggedFriends": [
     "54b235be6fd75df10c278b63",
     "5499ded286c27ff13a36b253"
   ],
   "userId": "5499ded286c27ff13a36b253",
   "userName": "Krasimir Tsonev",
   "date": ISODate("2015-02-08T20:54:18.137Z")
}
```

Now, let's update the fetching of the database records. We have the IDs of our friends, but we need their names. So, in the same content.js file, we will place the following code:

```
var numberOfPosts = result.length;
var friendsFetched = function() {
  numberOfPosts -= 1;
  if(numberOfPosts === 0) {
    response({
      posts: result
    }, res);
  }
}
result.forEach(function(value, index, arr) {
  arr[index].id = ObjectId(value._id);
  arr[index].ownPost = user._id.toString() ===
    ObjectId(arr[index].userId).toString();
  arr[index].numberOfLikes = arr[index].likes ?
    arr[index].likes.length : 0;
  delete arr[index].userId;
  delete arr[index]._id;
  getFriendsProfiles(db, arr[index].taggedFriends,
    function(friends) {
    arr[index].taggedFriends = friends;
    friendsFetched();
  });
});
```

We have the items from the database in the `results` array. The looping through the posts is still the same but doesn't send the response after the `forEach` call. For every post in the list, we need to send a request to the MongoDB database and get the name of the friends. So, we will initialize the `numberOfPosts` variable, and every time the request for the friend's name is finished, we will decrease the value. Once it gets to 0, we know that the last post is processed. After this, we will send the response to the browser.

Here is a small update of the `frontend/tpl/home.html` file that will make the `taggedFriends` array visible:

```
{{#each posts:index}}
  <div class="content-item">
    <h2>{{posts[index].userName}}</h2>
    {{posts[index].text}}
    {{#if posts[index].taggedFriends.length > 0}}
      <p>
        <small>
          Tagged: {{posts[index].taggedFriends.join(', ')}}
        </small>
      </p>
    {{/if}}
    {{#if posts[index].file}}
    <img src="/static/uploads/{{posts[index].file}}" />
    {{/if}}
  </div>
{{/each}}
```

Along with the owner, the text, and the picture (if any), we check whether there are any tagged people. If there are any tagged people, then we join all the elements of the `taggedFriends` array with the given separator. The result looks like the following screenshot:

Krasimir Tsonev

What a nice day. Isn't it?

Tagged: John Doe, Martin Greenstock

Sharing a post

The sharing function of our application will give an option to the current user to republish an already created post. We should make sure that the user does not share his/her own records. So, let's start from there. The API returns the posts and knows who created them. It also knows which user is making the request. The following code creates a new property called `ownPost`:

```
// backend/api/content.js
getCurrentUser(function(user) {
  ...
  getDatabaseConnection(function(db) {
    var collection = db.collection('content');
    collection.find({
      ...
    }).toArray(function(err, result) {
      result.forEach(function(value, index, arr) {
        arr[index].id = ObjectId(value._id);
        arr[index].ownPost = user._id.toString() ===
          ObjectId(arr[index].userId).toString();
        delete arr[index].userId;
        delete arr[index]._id;
      });
      response({ posts: result }, res);
    });
  });
}, req, res);
```

This is the logic that prepares the posts and sends them to the browser. The `getCurrentUser` property returns the user that is currently making the requests. The `user._id` variable is exactly what we need. This ID is actually assigned to the `userId` property for every post. So, we will simply compare them and determine whether the sharing is allowed or not. If the `ownPost` variable is equal to `true`, then the user should not be able to share the post.

In the previous section, we added a new markup to display the tagged friends. The space below them seems like a good place to place a **Share** button:

```
{{#if posts[index].taggedFriends.length > 0}}
  <p>
    <small>
      Tagged: {{posts[index].taggedFriends.join(', ')}}
    </small>
  </p>
{{/if}}
```

```
{{#if !posts[index].ownPost}}
<p><input type="button" value="Share"
on-click="share:{{posts[index].id}}" /></p>
{{/if}}
```

Here, the new `ownPost` property comes into use. If the post is not made by the current user, then we will show the button that dispatches the `share` event. Ractive.js gives us an opportunity to send data along with the event. In our case, this is the ID of the post.

The controller of the home page should listen to this event. A quick update of `controllers/Home.js` adds the listener, as follows:

```
this.on('share', function(e, id) {
  var formData = new FormData();
  formData.append('postId', id);
  model.sharePost(formData, getPosts);
});
```

The `model` object is an instance of the `ContentModel` class. The sharing is a new feature. So, we need to send queries to a different API endpoint. The new `sharePost` method looks like this:

```
// frontend/js/models/Content.js
sharePost: function(formData, callback) {
  var self = this;
  ajax.request({
    url: this.get('url') + '/share',
    method: 'POST',
    formData: formData,
    json: true
  })
  .done(function(result) {
    callback(null, result);
  })
  .fail(function(xhr) {
    callback(JSON.parse(xhr.responseText));
  });
}
```

We used some code that is similar to the preceding one many times in the previous chapter. It sends a `POST` request to the backend at a specific URL. Here, the URL is `/api/content/share`. It is also important to mention that `formData` contains the ID of the post that we want to share.

Let's continue and make the necessary changes in the API. We already defined the URL that will host this functionality — /api/content/share. A new route in backend/API.js is needed, which is as follows:

```
.add('api/content/share', require('./api/content-share'))
```

The next step involves the creation of the content-share controller. Like every other controller, we will start with requiring the helpers. We will skip this part and jump directly to the processing of the POST request:

```
// backend/api/content-share.js
case 'POST':
  var formidable = require('formidable');
  var form = new formidable.IncomingForm();
  form.parse(req, function(err, formData, files) {
    if(!formData.postId) {
      error('Please provide ID of a post.', res);
    } else {
      var done = function() {
        response({
          success: 'OK'
        }, res);
      };
      // ...
    }
  });
break;
```

The preceding method expects a postId variable. If there is no such variable, then we will respond with an error. The rest of the code again involves the usage of the formidable module and the defining of a done function to send a response for a successful operation. Here is the more interesting part:

```
getDatabaseConnection(function(db) {
  getCurrentUser(function(user) {
    var collection = db.collection('content');
    collection
    .find({ _id: ObjectId(formData.postId) })
    .toArray(function(err, result) {
      if(result.length === 0) {
        error('There is no post with that ID.', res);
      } else {
        var post = result[0];
        delete post._id;
        post.via = post.userName;
```

```
            post.userId = user ._id.toString();
            post.userName = user.firstName + ' ' + user.lastName;
            post.date = new Date();
            post.taggedFriends = [];
            collection.insert(post, done);
        }
    });
}, req, res);
```

After finding the post that should be shared, we will prepare an object that will be saved as a new record. We need to perform a few operations on the original post:

```
var post = result[0];
delete post._id;
post.via = post.userName;
post.userId = user ._id.toString();
post.userName = user.firstName + ' ' + user.lastName;
post.date = new Date();
post.taggedFriends = [];
collection.insert(post, done);
```

We surely do not need the _id property. MongoDB will create a new one. The third line defines a via property. We will talk about this in a minute, but in short, it is used to display the original author of the post. The lines after via set the owner of the new record. The date is also changed, and since this is a new post, we clear the taggedFriends array.

The shared post is now in the database and it is displayed in the users' feeds. Let's use the via property and show the original creator of the post in the following way:

```
// frontend/tpl/home.html
{{#each posts:index}}
<div class="content-item">
  <h2>{{posts[index].userName}}</h2>
  <p>{{posts[index].text}}</p>
  {{#if posts[index].via}}
  <small>via {{posts[index].via}}</small>
  {{/if}}
  ...
```

We will check whether the variable is available and if it is, then we will add a small text below the text of the post. The result will look like this:

John Doe

What a nice day. Isn't it?

via Krasimir Tsonev

Liking posts and counting the number of likes

The users of our social network should be able to see a **Like** button. By clicking on it, they will send a request to the API and our task is to count these clicks. Of course, only one click per user is allowed. As in the previous section, we will start by updating the user interface. Let's add another button next to the **Share** one in the following way:

```
// frontend/tpl/home.html
<input type="button" value="Like"
on-click="like:{{posts[index].id}}" />
{{#if !posts[index].ownPost}}
<input type="button" value="Share"
on-click="share:{{posts[index].id}}" />
{{/if}}
```

The new button dispatches a `like` event, and we will again pass the ID of the post. It is actually similar to the `share` event. Also, the liking action will use the same type of communication with the backend. So, it makes sense to refactor our code and use only one function for both the features. In the previous section, we added the `sharePost` method to the `models/Content.js` file. Let's change it to `usePost` in the following way:

```
usePost: function(url, formData, callback) {
  var self = this;
  ajax.request({
    url: this.get('url') + '/' + url,
    method: 'POST',
```

```
      formData: formData,
      json: true
   })
   .done(function(result) {
     callback(null, result);
   })
   .fail(function(xhr) {
     callback(JSON.parse(xhr.responseText));
   });
}
```

Because the only one thing that differs is the URL, we define it as a parameter. The `formData` interface still contains the ID of the post. Here is the updated code of our controller:

```
// controllers/Home.js
this.on('share', function(e, id) {
  var formData = new FormData();
  formData.append('postId', id);
  model.usePost('share', formData, getPosts);
});
this.on('like', function(e, id) {
  var formData = new FormData();
  formData.append('postId', id);
  model.usePost('like', formData, getPosts);
});
```

We skipped the definition of one more method and made the implementation of the model a bit more flexible. We may need to add a new operation and the last tweak will come in handy.

According to the changes in the API, we followed the same workflow. A new route responding to `/api/content/like` is needed, which can be created as follows:

```
// backend/API.js
add('api/content/like', require('./api/content-like'))
```

The `content-like` controller still does not exist. We will create a new `backend/api/content-like.js` file that will host the logic related to the liking. The usual things like protecting the method from unauthorized users and fetching the POST data with `formidable` are present. This time, we are not going to use the `insert` method of the collection. Instead, we will use `update`. We will construct a slightly more complex MongoDB query and update a new property called `likes`.

The `update` method accepts four parameters. The first one is the criteria. The records that match our criteria will be updated. The second one contains instructions with regards to what we want to update. The third parameter contains additional options and the last one is a callback that is invoked once the operation ends. Here is how our query looks:

```
getDatabaseConnection(function(db) {
  getCurrentUser(function(user) {
    var collection = db.collection('content');
    var userName = user.firstName + ' ' + user.lastName;
    collection.update(
      {
        $and: [
          { _id: ObjectId(formData.postId) },
          { "likes.user": { $nin: [userName] } }
        ]
      },
      {
        $push: {
          likes: { user: userName }
        }
      },
      {w:1},
      function(err) {
        done();
      }
    );
  }, req, res);
});
```

The code is indeed a bit long but it does its job. Let's go through it line by line. The first parameter, our criteria, makes sure that we are going to update the right post. Because we use the `$and` operator, the second object in the array should also be valid. You may notice that a few lines below `$and`, the `$push` operator adds a new object to an array called `likes`. Every object has a `name` property containing the name of the user that hits the **Like** button. So, in our `"likes.user": { $nin: [userName] }` criteria, it means that the record will be updated only if `userName` is not in some of the elements of the `likes` array. This might look a little complex, but it is really a powerful combination of operators. Without this, we would probably end up making several queries to the database.

The {w: 1} option always changes its value if a callback is passed.

Once the record is updated, we will simply call the done method and send a response to the user.

With the changes in the API, we successfully finished this feature. Here is how a post looks in the browser now:

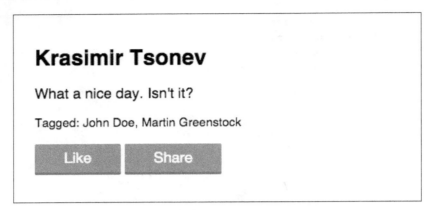

Showing the number of likes

We keep the likes in an array. It is easy to count the elements there and find out how many times a post is liked. We will make two small changes that will make this possible. The first one is in the API, which is the place where we prepare the post objects:

```
// backend/api/content.js
result.forEach(function(value, index, arr) {
  arr[index].id = ObjectId(value._id);
  arr[index].ownPost = user._id.toString() ===
    ObjectId(arr[index].userId).toString();
  arr[index].numberOfLikes = arr[index].likes ?
    arr[index].likes.length : 0;
  delete arr[index].userId;
  delete arr[index]._id;
});
```

A new `numberOfLikes` property is attached. The records did not have a `likes` property in the beginning. So, we have to check whether it exists before we use it. If we have `numberOfLikes` variable, we can update the label of the **Like** button in the frontend to the following code:

```
<input type="button" value="Like ({{posts[index].numberOfLikes}})"
    on-click="like:{{posts[index].id}}" />
```

Once created, every post has zero likes. So, the label of the button is **Like (0)**, but after the first click, it changes to **Like (1)**. The following screenshot demonstrates how this looks in practice:

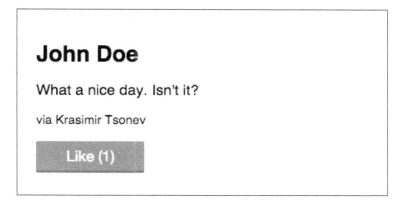

Summary

This chapter was about some of the most used features in social networks nowadays—tagging, sharing, and liking. We updated both sides of our application and validated our knowledge from the previous chapters.

The next chapter will be about real-time communication. We will build a chat window for our users, and they will be able to send real-time messages to others.

10
Adding Real-time Chat

In the previous two chapters, we extended our social network by adding new features to create pages and share posts. In this chapter, we will discuss real-time communication between users in the system. The technology that we are going to use is called WebSockets. The plan for this part of the book is as follows:

- Getting to know WebSockets
- Bringing Socket.IO to the project
- Preparing the UI of the chat area
- Exchanging messages between the client and the server
- Sending messages to the user's friends only
- Customizing the output of the chat

Getting to know WebSockets

WebSockets is a technology that opens a two-way (bidirectional) interactive channel between the server and the browser. By using this type of communication, we are able to exchange messages without the need of an initial request. Both sides simply dispatch events to each other. The other benefits of WebSockets are lower bandwidth requirement and latency.

There are a couple of ways to transfer data from the server to the client and vice versa. Let's check the most popular ones and see why WebSockets is considered the best option for real-time web apps:

- **Classic HTTP communication**: The client requests a resource from the server. The server figures out what the response should be and sends it. In the context of real-time applications, this is not very practical because we have to manually ask for more data.

- **Ajax polling**: It is similar to the classical HTTP request except for the fact that we have the code that constantly sends requests to the server, for instance, in an interval of half a second. This is not really a good idea because our server will receive a huge amount of requests.

- **Ajax long-polling**: We again have a client that performs HTTP requests, but this time, the server delays the result and does not respond immediately. It waits till there is new information available and then answers the request.

- **HTML5 Server-sent Events (EventSource)**: In this type of communication, we have a channel from the server to the client and the server automatically sends data to the browser. This technique is used mostly when we need a one-directional data flow.

- **WebSockets**: As mentioned before, if we use WebSockets, we have a two-way (bidirectional) data flow. Both sides, the client and the server, can send messages without asking the other side.

Server-sent Events may work in some cases, but for real-time chat, we definitely need WebSockets because we want users to be able to send messages to each other. The solution to this that we will implement looks like the following screenshot:

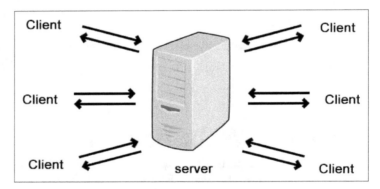

Every user will connect to the server and start sending messages. Our backend will be in charge of distributing the messages to the rest of the users.

Working with the raw WebSockets API may be not so easy. In the next section, we will introduce a really helpful Node.js module to deal with WebSockets.

Bringing Socket.IO to the project

Socket.IO (`http://socket.io/`) is a real-time engine built on the top of WebSockets technology. It is a layer that makes web development easy and straightforward. Like every new thing nowadays, WebSockets comes with its own problems. Not every browser supports this technology. We may have problems with the protocol and missing events such as heartbeats, timeouts, or disconnection support. Thankfully, Socket.IO fixes these issues. It even provides fallbacks for the browsers that do not support WebSockets and goes with techniques such as long-polling.

Before making changes in our backend, we need to install the module. The engine is distributed in the same way as every other Node.js module; it is available via the package manager. So, we have to add Socket.IO to the `package.json` file in the following way:

```
{
  "name": "nodejs-by-example",
  "version": "0.0.2",
  "description": "Node.js by example",
  "scripts": {
    "start": "node server.js"
  },
  "dependencies": {
    "socket.io": "1.3.3"
    ...
    ...
  }
}
```

After that change, we will run `npm install` and get the `node_modules/socket.io` folder populated. Having installed the module, we can start updating our social network. Let's add a `Chat.js` file to the backend directory containing the following code:

```
module.exports = function(app) {
  var io = require('socket.io')(app);
  io.on('connection', function (socket) {
    socket.emit('news', { hello: 'world' });
    socket.on('my other event', function (data) {
      console.log(data);
    });
  });
}
```

The new module exports a function that accepts the HTTP server. In `server.js`, we can initialize it by using `http.createServer`, as follows:

```
var app = http.createServer(checkSession).listen(port, '127.0.0.1');
console.log("Listening on 127.0.0.1:" + port);

var Chat = require('./backend/Chat');
Chat(app);
```

Socket.IO is entirely built on the concept of event firing and listening. The `io` variable represents our communication hub. Every time a new user connects to our server, we get a connection event, and the handler that is invoked receives a `socket` object that we will use to process messages from and to the browser.

In the preceding example, we sent (`emit`) an event with the `news` name containing some simple data. After this, we started listening to the other event that would come from the client.

Now, even if we restart the server, we are not going to receive any socket connections. This is because we did not change the frontend code. In order to make Socket.IO work on the client side, we need to include the `/socket.io/socket.io.js` file in our pages. The layout of our application is stored in `backend/tpl/page.html`, and after the modification, it looks like this:

```
<!doctype html>
<html lang="en">
<head>
  <meta charset="utf-8">
  <title>Node.js by example</title>
  <meta http-equiv="Content-Type" content="text/html;
    charset=utf-8" />
  <meta name="description" content="Node.js by examples">
  <meta name="author" content="Packt">
  <link rel="stylesheet" href="/static/css/styles.css">
</head>
<body>
  <div class="container"></div>
  <script src="/socket.io/socket.io.js"></script>
  <script src="/static/js/ractive.js"></script>
  <script src="/static/js/app.js"></script>
</body>
</html>
```

The `socket.io.js` file does not exist in our codebase. It is a part of the Socket.IO module. The engine automatically registers a route to it and takes care that it serves the file.

The final step in the testing of our WebSockets implementation is the connecting to the server. For the sake of simplicity, let's add a few lines of code to the `frontend/js/app.js` file:

```
window.onload = function() {

    ...

    var socket = io('http://localhost:9000');
    socket.on('news', function (data) {
      console.log(data);
      socket.emit('my other event', { my: 'data' });
    });

};
```

We will put our code in the `onload` handler because we want to make sure that all the external JavaScript files are fully loaded. Then, we will initialize a connection to `http://localhost:9000`, which is the same host and port that the Node.js server runs on. The rest of the code does only one thing—it listens for a `news` event and responds with the other event message. If we run the server and load `http://localhost:9000` in a browser, we will get the following result in the terminal:

```
node server.js
Listening on 127.0.0.1:9000
{ my: 'data' }
```

We got `{ my: 'data' }` as an output because we have `console.log(data)` in the `backend/Chat.js` file.

Preparing the UI of the chat area

Because real-time chat is an important part of our social network, we will create a separate page for it. As we did in the previous chapters, we will start with a new link in the main navigation, as follows:

```
<nav>
  <ul>
    <li><a on-click="goto:home">Home</a></li>
    {{#if !isLogged }}
      <li><a on-click="goto:register">Register</a></li>
      <li><a on-click="goto:login">Login</a></li>
    {{else}}
      <li class="right"><a on-click="goto:logout">Logout</a></li>
      <li class="right"><a
```

```
        on-click="goto:profile">Profile</a></li>
      <li class="right"><a on-click="goto:find-friends">Find
        friends</a></li>
      <li class="right"><a on-click="goto:pages">Pages</a></li>
      <li class="right"><a on-click="goto:chat">Chat</a></li>
    {{/if}}
  </ul>
</nav>
```

The latest link in the list will forward the user to the `http://localhost:9000/chat` URL where he/she will see the interface of the chat.

Let's handle the `/chat` route by tweaking the `frontend/js/app.js` file. Let's make another addition to our router, as follows:

```
Router
...
...
.add('chat', function() {
  if(userModel.isLogged()) {
    var p = new Chat();
    showPage(p);
  } else {
    Router.navigate('login');
  }
})
.add(function() {
  Router.navigate('home');
})
.listen()
.check();
```

In the same file, we will require the `frontend/js/controllers/Chat.js` module. It will contain the chat logic in the client side. We will start with something simple—a basic Ractive.js component, which can be implemented as follows:

```
// frontend/js/controllers/Chat.js
module.exports = Ractive.extend({
  template: require('../../tpl/chat'),
  components: {
    navigation: require('../views/Navigation'),
    appfooter: require('../views/Footer')
  },
  data: {
    output: ''
  },
  onrender: function() {

  }
});
```

Like every other controller in our application, Chat.js has an associated template that contains an empty <div> element to display chat messages, a text field, and a button to send data to the server:

```
// front/tpl/chat.html
<header>
  <navigation></navigation>
</header>
<div class="hero">
  <h1>Chat</h1>
</div>
<form>
  <div class="chat-output">{{output}}</div>
  <input type="text" value="{{text}}" />
  <a href="#" on-click="send" class="button">Send</a>
</form>
<appfooter />
```

It is worth a mentioning that if you want to update the content of the chat-output element, you need to change the value of the output variable. The button also dispatches a send event, and we will catch this in the next section. After the compilation of the assets, if you go to the chat's URL, you will see the following screen:

Exchanging messages between the client and the server

We are ready to write some working Socket.IO code. So far, we placed code snippets that only proved that the socket connection works. For example, the code that was added to `frontend/js/app.js` should be moved to `frontend/js/controllers/Chat.js`, which is the controller responsible for the chat page. Because it acts as a base for this real-time feature, we will start from there. Let's add a couple of local variables to the component, as follows:

```
data: {
  messages: ['Loading. Please wait.'],
  output: '',
  socketConnected: false
}
```

These variables have default values, and they are available in the component's template. The first one, `messages`, will keep all the messages that come from the users in the chat, including the current user. The `output` variable is used to populate the message container on the screen. The last one, `socketConnected`, controls the visibility of the text field and the button. If it is set to `false`, the controls will be hidden. Before initializing the connection with the server or getting disconnected for some reason, it is better to hide the chat input text field until the connection with the server is initialized. Otherwise, we may get disconnected for some reason. Here is how the updated template looks:

```
// frontend/tpl/chat.html
<header>
  <navigation></navigation>
</header>
<div class="hero">
  <h1>Chat</h1>
</div>
<form>
  <div class="chat-output"
    data-component="output">{{{output}}}</div>
  {{#if socketConnected}}
    <input type="text" value="{{text}}" />
    <a href="#" on-click="send" class="button">Send</a>
  {{/if}}
</form>
<appfooter />
```

The difference is the {{if}} operator that wraps the field and the button. At the end of the chapter, we will colorize the messages, and we will be required to pass HTML tags. We will use {{{output}}} instead of {{output}} so that the framework displays them correctly (by turning off autoescaping).

Let's go back to the frontend controller. We mentioned that the code placed in app.js moves here. It was the actual connection to the socket server. We will extend it in the following way:

```
var self = this;
var socket = io('http://localhost:9000');
socket.on('connect', function() {
  self.push('messages', 'Connected!');
  self.set('socketConnected', true);
  self.find('input[type="text"]').focus();
});
socket.on('disconnect', function() {
  self.set('socketConnected', false);
  self.push('messages', 'Disconnected!');
});
socket.on('server-talking', function(data) {
  self.push('messages', data.text);
});
```

After receiving the connect event, we will add the Connected! string to the messages array. So, after receiving the **Loading. Please wait.** message, the user will see a confirmation that informs him/her that the application has established a successful socket connection. By setting socketConnected to true, we reveal the input controls and give an option to the user to send chat messages. The last thing in this handler is forcing the browser to focus on the input field, a nice little detail that saves a mouse click of the user.

The socket object may dispatch another event—disconnect. There are two actions that we can take in this situation—hiding the input controls and notifying the user by showing the Disconnected! string in the browser.

The last event that we were listening to was server-talking. This is our own event—a message that our backend code will dispatch. In the beginning, the data object will contain only one text property, which will be the chat message. We will simply append it to the rest of the elements of the messages array.

The lines that we talked about earlier listen to the events that come from the backend. Let's write some code that sends information from the client to the server:

```
var send = function() {
  socket.emit('client-talking', { text: self.get('text')});
  self.set('text', '');
}
this.on('send', send);
```

The `send` function is called when the user clicks the button. We use the same `socket` object and its `emit` method to transfer the text to the server. We also clear the content of the input field so that the user can start composing a new message. Pressing the button every time is probably annoying. The following code triggers the `send` function when the user presses the *Enter* key:

```
this.find('form').addEventListener('keypress', function(e) {
  if(e.keyCode === 13 && e.target.nodeName === 'INPUT') {
    e.preventDefault();
    send();
  }
});
```

The `this.find` method returns a valid DOM element. We attach the `keypress` listener to the `form` element because the `input` variable is not always visible. Thanks to events bubbling, we are able to catch the event in the upper element. It is also worth a mention that in some browsers, a different code is required to listen to DOM events.

The last thing that we have to take care of is the displaying of the content of the `messages` array on the screen. If you check the code that we've written so far, you will see that we did not update the `output` variable. Here is a new component method that will handle this:

```
updateOutput: function() {
  this.set('output', this.get('messages').join('<br />'));
  var outputEl = this.find('[data-component="output"]');
  outputEl.scrollTop = outputEl.scrollHeight;
}
```

Instead of looping through all the elements of the array, we use the `join` method. It joins all the elements of the array into a string separated by the given parameter. In our case, we need a new line after every message. Once we start receiving more data, we will need to scroll the `<div>` element down so that the user sees the latest ones. The other two lines of the function position the scroller of the container at the bottom.

The `updateOutput` function should be called once a new message arrives. The Ractive.js observing is perfect for such cases:

```
this.observe('messages', this.updateOutput);
```

Only one line is needed to wire the updating of a `messages` array to the `updateOutput` method. After this addition, every `push` to the message array will force the render of the `chat-output` element.

The code for the component is as follows:

```
module.exports = Ractive.extend({
  template: require('../../tpl/chat'),
  components: {
    navigation: require('../views/Navigation'),
    appfooter: require('../views/Footer')
  },
  data: {
    messages: ['Loading. Please wait.'],
    output: '',
    socketConnected: false
  },
  onrender: function() {

    var self = this;
    var socket = io('http://localhost:9000');
    socket.on('connect', function() {
      self.push('messages', 'Connected!');
      self.set('socketConnected', true);
      self.find('input[type="text"]').focus();
    });
    socket.on('disconnect', function() {
      self.set('socketConnected', false);
      self.push('messages', 'Disconnected!');
    });
    socket.on('server-talking', function(data) {
      self.push('messages', data.text);
    });

    var send = function() {
      socket.emit('client-talking', { text: self.get('text')});
      self.set('text', '');
    }
```

```
        this.on('send', send);
        this.observe('messages', this.updateOutput);

        this.find('form').addEventListener('keypress', function(e) {
            if(e.keyCode === 13 && e.target.nodeName === 'INPUT') {
                e.preventDefault();
                send();
            }
        });

    },
    updateOutput: function() {
        this.set('output', this.get('messages').join('<br />'));
        var outputEl = this.find('[data-component="output"]');
        outputEl.scrollTop = outputEl.scrollHeight;
    }
});
```

The frontend is ready to send and receive messages through the socket. However, the backend still contains the initial example code that we started with. A small update of the Chat module will make it possible to send messages to the users:

```
// backend/Code.js
module.exports = function(app) {
    var io = require('socket.io')(app);
    io.on('connection', function (socket) {
        socket.on('client-talking', function (data) {
            io.sockets.emit('server-talking', { text: data.text });
        });
    });
}
```

We are still listening for the connection event. The socket object that we receive in the handler represents the connection with the user. After this, we will start listening to the client-talking event that is dispatched by the frontend when the user types something in a field or presses the button or the *Enter* key. Once the data is received, we broadcast it to all the users in the system. The io.sockets.emit variable sends a message to all the clients who are currently using the server.

Sending messages to the user's friends only

The last change in our backend dispatches the received chat messages to all the users in our social network. This is of course not really practical, because we may exchange text with people who do not know each other. We have to change our code accordingly so that we send messages only to the users in our friends list.

With Socket.IO, we do not have access to the `request` and `response` objects as we do in the backend API by default. This will make the solving of the problem a bit more interesting because we can't recognize the user sending the message. Thankfully, Socket.IO gives us access to the active session. It is in a raw format. So, we will need to parse it and extract the user's profile data. To do this, we will use the `cookie` Node.js module. Let's add it to the `package.json` file in the following way:

```
"dependencies": {
  "cookie": "0.1.2",
  "socket.io": "1.3.3",
  . . .
  . . .
}
```

With another `npm install` in the terminal, we will be able to `require` the module. In *Chapter 8, Creating Pages and Events,* we refactored our API and created the `backend/api/helpers.js` file that contains utility functions. We will add another file similar to `getCurrentUser` by using only the `session` object, as follows:

```
var getCurrentUserBySessionObj = function(callback, obj) {
  getDatabaseConnection(function(db) {
    var collection = db.collection('users');
    collection.find({
      email: obj.user.email
    }).toArray(function(err, result) {
      if(result.length === 0) {
        callback({ error: 'No user found.' });
      } else {
        callback(null, result[0]);
      }
    });
  });
};
```

If we compare both methods, we will see that there are two differences. The first difference is that we do not receive the usual request and response objects; we receive only a callback and a `session` object. The second change is that the result is always sent to the callback even if it is an error.

Armed with the `getCurrentUserBySessionObj` function, we can modify `backend/Chat.js` so that it sends messages only to the friends of the current user. Let's initialize the needed helpers first. We will add the following lines to the top of the file:

```
var helpers = require('./api/helpers');
var getCurrentUserBySessionObj =
  helpers.getCurrentUserBySessionObj;
var cookie = require('cookie');
```

We already talked about the `cookie` module. The session data that is available throughout the Socket.IO engine is reachable through `socket.request.headers.cookie`. If we print the value in the console, we will get something like the following screenshot:

io=Lc4uEqHxT4DhkFvRAAAB; csrftoken=laxBMLcoDnys4WosDR1JS0ThV9MxIX85; express:s
ess=eyJ1c2VyIjp7ImZpcnN0TmFtZSI6IktyYXNpbWlyIiwibGFzdE5hbWUiOiJUc29uZXYiLCJlbW
FpbCI6ImFAYS5jb20iLCJmcmllbmRzIjpbIjU0YjIzNWJlNmZkNzVkZjEwYzI30GI2MyIsIjU0YjIz
NjMwNmZkNzVkZjEwYzI30GI2NyIsIjU0YjIzMzJmN2QyYjU3MjMwYWE2NDYxOCJdfX0=; express:
sess.sig=UAMvPMw_Il35QpJSXubHJE64gMY

The preceding output is a Base64-encoded string that we definitely cannot directly use. Thankfully, Node.js has interfaces to easily decode such values. Here is a short function that will extract the needed JSON object:

```
var decode = function(string) {
  var body = new Buffer(string, 'base64').toString('utf8');
  return JSON.parse(body);
};
```

We passed the string from the cookie and received the normal `user` object that we will later use in `getCurrentUserBySessionObj`.

So, we have mechanisms to find out who the current user is and who his/her friends are. All we have to do is cache the available socket connections and associated users. We will introduce a new global (for the module) `users` variable. It will act as a hash map where the key will be the ID of the user and the value will contain the socket and the friends. In order to broadcast messages to the right users, we can summarize the logic in the following method:

```
var broadcastMessage = function(userId, message) {
  var user = users[userId];
  if(user && user.friends && user.friends.length > 0) {
    user.socket.emit('server-talking', { text: message });
    for(var i=0; i<user.friends.length; i++) {
      var friend = users[user.friends[i]];
      if(friend && friend.socket) {
        friend.socket.emit('server-talking', { text: message });
      }
    }
  }
};
```

This code provides a function that accepts the ID of a user and the text message. We will first check whether a socket reference is cached. If it is, then we will make sure that the user has friends. If this is valid too, then we will start dispatching messages. The first `emit` item is to the user himself/herself so that he/she receives his/her own message. The rest of the code loops over the friends and sends the text to all of them.

We, of course, have to update the code that accepts the socket connection. Here is the new version of the same:

```
module.exports = function(app) {
  var io = require('socket.io')(app);
  io.on('connection', function (socket) {
    var sessionData = cookie.parse(socket.request.headers.cookie);
    sessionData = decode(sessionData['express:sess']);
    if(sessionData && sessionData.user) {
      getCurrentUserBySessionObj(function(err, user) {
        var userId = user._id.toString();
        users[userId] = {
          socket: socket,
          friends: user.friends
        };
        socket.on('client-talking', function (data) {
          broadcastMessage(userId, data.text);
        });
        socket.on('disconnect', function() {
          users[userId] = null;
        });
```

```
      }, sessionData);
    }

  });
}
```

We will now fetch the cookie value and determine the current user. The `socket` object and the user's friends are cached. Then, we will continue listening for the `client-talking` event, but now, we will send messages via the `broadcastMessage` function. A small but very important addition is made towards the end; we listen for the `disconnect` event and remove the cached data. That is needed to prevent sending data to the disconnected users.

Customizing the output of the chat

It is nice that we can send messages to the right people, but the chat is still a bit confusing because every text message that appears on the screen is in the same color and we don't know which of our friends sent it. In this section, we are going to make two improvements—we will append the user's name to the front of the message and colorize the text.

Let's start with the colors and add a new helper method to the `backend/api/helpers.js` file:

```
var getRandomColor = function() {
  var letters = '0123456789ABCDEF'.split('');
  var color = '#';
  for(var i = 0; i < 6; i++ ) {
    color += letters[Math.floor(Math.random() * 16)];
  }
  return color;
}
```

The following function generates a valid RGB color that is ready for use in CSS. The right moment for you to pick a color for the user is when you cache the `socket` object, as follows:

```
...
var getRandomColor = helpers.getRandomColor;

module.exports = function(app) {
  var io = require('socket.io')(app);
  io.on('connection', function (socket) {
    var sessionData = cookie.parse(socket.request.headers.cookie);
    sessionData = decode(sessionData['express:sess']);
    if(sessionData && sessionData.user) {
      getCurrentUserBySessionObj(function(err, user) {
```

```
        var userId = user._id.toString();
        users[userId] = {
          socket: socket,
          friends: user.friends,
          color: getRandomColor()
        };
        socket.on('client-talking', function (data) {
          broadcastMessage(user, data.text);
        });
        socket.on('disconnect', function() {
          users[userId] = null;
        });
      }, sessionData);
    }

  });
}
```

So, along with the socket object and friends, we store a randomly picked color. There is another small update. We no longer pass the user's ID to the broadcastMessage function. We send the whole object because we need to fetch the first and last name of the user.

Here is the updated broadcastMessage helper:

```
var broadcastMessage = function(userProfile, message) {
  var user = users[userProfile._id.toString()];
  var userName = userProfile.firstName + ' ' +
   userProfile.lastName;
  if(user && user.friends && user.friends.length > 0) {
    user.socket.emit('server-talking', {
      text: message,
      user: userName,
      color: user.color
    });
    for(var i=0; i<user.friends.length; i++) {
      var friend = users[user.friends[i]];
      if(friend && friend.socket) {
        friend.socket.emit('server-talking', {
          text: message,
          user: userName,
          color: user.color
        });
      }
    }
  }
};
```

Now, the `data` object that goes to the client contains two additional properties — the name of the current user and his/her randomly picked color.

The backend does its job. All we have to do now is tweak the frontend controller so that it uses the name and color, as follows:

```
// frontend/js/controllers/Chat.js
socket.on('server-talking', function(data) {
  var message = '<span style="color:' + data.color + '">';
  message += data.user + ': ' + data.text;
  message += '</span>';
  self.push('messages', message);
});
```

Instead of sending only text, we wrap the message in a `<span>` tag. It has a text color applied. Also, the message starts with the name of the user.

The final result of our work looks like the following screenshot:

Summary

Socket.IO is one of the most popular Node.js tools used to develop real-time applications. In this chapter, we successfully used it to build an interactive chat. The users in our network were able to not only post content that appeared in their feeds but also exchange messages with other users in real time. The WebSockets technology made this possible.

The next chapter is dedicated to testing. We will learn about a few popular modules that will help us write tests.

11
Testing the User Interface

In *Chapter 10, Adding Real-time Chat*, we extended our social network by adding a real-time chat function. We used WebSockets and Socket.IO in particular to implement the communication between the users in our system. The last chapter of this book is dedicated to user interface testing. We will explore two popular tools to run headless browser testing. This chapter covers the following topics:

- Introducing the basic testing toolset
- Preparing our project to run tests
- Running our tests with PhantomJS
- Testing the user's registration
- Testing with DalekJS

Introducing the basic testing toolset

Before writing the tests, we will spend some time talking about the testing toolset. We need some instruments to define and run our tests.

The testing framework

In the context of JavaScript, the testing framework is a set of functions that help you organize the tests into logical groups. There are framework functions such as `suite`, `describe`, `test`, or `it` that define the structure of our suite. Here is a short example:

```
describe('Testing database communication', function () {
  it('should connect to the database', function(done) {
    // the actual testing goes here
  });
  it('should execute a query', function(done) {
    // the actual testing goes here
  });
});
```

We used the `describe` function to wrap the more detailed tests (`it`) into a group. Organizing the group in such a way helps us keep focus and at the same time, it is quite informative.

Some popular testing frameworks in the JavaScript community are **QUnit**, **Jasmine**, and **Mocha**.

The assertion library

What we usually do while testing is run an assertion. We very often compare the values of variables to check whether they match with what we expected when we originally wrote the program's logic. Some testing frameworks come with their own assertion library, some don't.

The following line shows a simple usage of such a library:

```
expect(10).to.be.a('number')
```

It is important to mention that the APIs are designed like this so that we understand the context by reading the test.

Node.js even has its own built-in library called `assert`. Some of the other options are **Chai**, **Expect**, and **Should.js**.

Runner

The runner is a tool that we use to execute the test in a specific context, which is very often a specific browser, but it may also be a different operating system or customized environment. We may or may not need a runner. In this particular chapter, we will use DalekJS as the test runner.

Preparing our project to run tests

Now we know what tools we need to run our tests. The next step is to prepare our project to place such tests. Normally during development, we test our application by visiting the pages and interacting with them. We know the result of these actions and we verify if everything is okay. We want to do the same thing with automated tests. However, instead of us repeating the same steps again and again, there will be a script.

In order to make these scripts work, we have to put them in the right context. In other words, they should be executed in the context of our application.

In the previous section, we mentioned Chai (an assertion library) and Mocha (a testing framework). They play well together. So, we will add them to our list of dependencies, as follows:

```
// package.json

...

"dependencies": {
    "chai": "2.0.0",
    "mocha": "2.1.0",
    ...
}

...
```

A quick run of `npm install` will set up the modules in the `node_modules` directory. Chai and Mocha are distributed as Node.js modules, but we may use them in the browser environment, too. The newly created folders in `node_modules` contain compiled versions. For example, to run Mocha in the browser, we have to include `node_modules/mocha/mocha.js` in our page.

Our social network is a single-page application. We have a main HTML template that is served by the backend, which is located in `backend/tpl/page.html`. The Node.js server reads this file and sends it to the browser. The rest is handled by the JavaScript code. Here is how `page.html` looks:

```html
<!doctype html>
<html lang="en">
<head>
  <meta charset="utf-8">
  <title>Node.js by example</title>
  <meta http-equiv="Content-Type" content="text/html;
    charset=utf-8" />
  <meta name="description" content="Node.js by example">
  <meta name="author" content="Packt">
  <link rel="stylesheet" href="/static/css/styles.css">
</head>
<body>
  <div class="container"></div>
  <script src="/socket.io/socket.io.js"></script>
  <script src="/static/js/ractive.js"></script>
  <script src="/static/js/app.js"></script>
</body>
</html>
```

The file contains all the external resources needed to run the application. However, now we need to add a few more tags; some of them are as follows:

- The `/node_modules/mocha/mocha.css` file contains styles for the proper display of the results of the tests. This is a part of Mocha's reporters.

- The `/node_modules/mocha/mocha.js` file is the testing framework.

- The `/node_modules/chai/chai.js` file is the assertion library.

- The `/tests/spec.js` is a file that contains the actual test. It still does not exist. We will create a `tests` directory and a `spec.js` file inside it.

- An empty `div` tag acts as a placeholder for the test results and a few lines of JavaScript bootstrap the Mocha framework.

We can't add all these new elements in the current `page.html` file, because the users of the system will see them. We will place them in another file and tweak the backend so that it serves it under specific conditions. Let's create `backend/tpl/pageTest.html`:

```
<!doctype html>
<html lang="en">
<head>
  ...
  <link rel="stylesheet" href="/static/css/styles.css">
  <link rel="stylesheet" href="/node_modules/mocha/mocha.css" />
</head>
<body>
  <div class="container"></div>
  <script src="/socket.io/socket.io.js"></script>
  <script src="/static/js/ractive.js"></script>
  <script src="/static/js/app.js"></script>

  <div id="mocha"></div>
  <script src="/node_modules/mocha/mocha.js"></script>
  <script src="/node_modules/chai/chai.js"></script>
  <script>
    mocha.ui('bdd');
    mocha.reporter('html');
    expect = chai.expect;
  </script>
  <script src="/tests/spec.js"></script>
  <script>
    if (window.mochaPhantomJS) {
      mochaPhantomJS.run();
    }
```

```
      else {
        mocha.run();
      }
    </script>

  </body>
  </html>
```

Once `mocha.js` and `chai.js` are injected in the page, we will configure the framework. Our user interface will follow behavior-driven development and the reporter will be `html`. Mocha has several types of reporters, and since we wanted to display the results in a browser, we used this one. We defined an `expect` global object that played the role of an assertion tool.

The lines after that will come in handy in the next section where we will run our test with PhantomJS. These lines will basically check whether there is a `window.mochaPhantomJS` object, and if there is, it will be used instead of the default `mocha`.

So far, so good. We have instruments that will help us to run and write our test and a page that contains the necessary code. The next step is to tweak the backend so that it uses the new `pageTest.html` file:

```
// backend/Default.js
var fs = require('fs');
var url = require('url');

var html = fs.readFileSync(__dirname +
  '/tpl/page.html').toString('utf8');
var htmlWithTests = fs.readFileSync(__dirname +
  '/tpl/pageTest.html').toString('utf8');

module.exports = function(req, res) {
  res.writeHead(200, {'Content-Type': 'text/html'});
  var urlParts = url.parse(req.url, true);
  var parameters = urlParts.query;
  if(typeof parameters.test !== 'undefined') {
    res.end(htmlWithTests + '\n');
  } else {
    res.end(html + '\n');
  }
}
```

The file that we have to change is `Default.js`. That's the handler of the `Default.js` file's route in our application. The newly added `htmlWithTests` variable contains the new HTML markup. We use the `url` module to find out the GET variables that come from the client. If there is a `test` parameter, then we will load the page containing the layout and the test. Otherwise, it is the original HTML.

After the last change, we can run the server and open `http://localhost:9000/register?test=1`. However, we will get a bunch of error messages complaining that there are some missing files. This happens because the `server.js` file does not recognize URLs that start with `node_modules` or `tests`. The files that exist in these directories are static resources. So, we can use the already defined `Assets` module, as follows:

```
// server.js
...
Router
.add('static', Assets)
.add('node_modules', Assets)
.add('tests', Assets)
.add('api', API)
.add(Default);
```

Finally, there is a file left that we have to create—`tests/spec.js`:

```
describe("Testing", function () {
  it("Test case", function (done) {
    expect(1).to.be.equal(1);
    done();
  });
});
```

This code is the simplest structure of a test. We have a group and a test inside. The key moment here is to run `done()` towards the end of the test.

We know that this test passes. The result in the browser looks like the following screenshot:

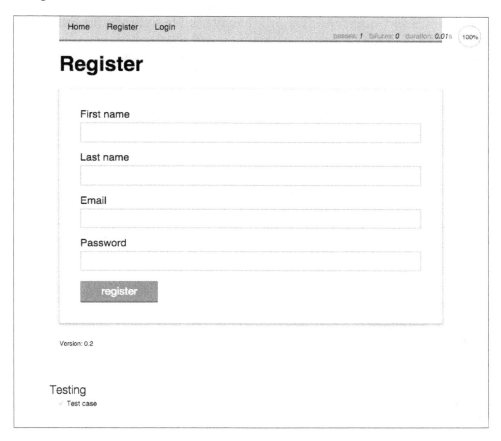

It is worth mentioning that the loaded page is still the same except for the elements in the top-right corner and below the footer. These new tags are generated by the Mocha framework. This is how the `html` reporter displays the results of our test.

Running our test with PhantomJS

The result of the preceding sections is an automated test that runs in the browser. However, this is very often not enough. We may need to integrate the testing in our deployment processes, and using the browser is not always an option. Thankfully, there is a type of browser called a **headless browser**. It is a functional browser without a user interface. We still can visit a page, click links, or fill forms, but all of these actions are controlled by code. This is perfect for us and for automated testing.

There are a couple of popular headless browsers. Selenium (`https://github.com/seleniumhq/selenium`) is one of them. It is well documented and has a big community. Another one is PhantomJS. It plays well with Node.js. So we are going to use it.

We already have several components added to the test environment. To use PhantomJS directly, some supplementary configuration is needed. In order to avoid additional complexity, we will install the `mocha-phantomjs` module. Its purpose is to simplify the usage of the headless browser, especially in a combination of the Mocha framework. The following command will set `mocha-phantomjs` as a global command in our terminal:

```
npm install mocha-phantomjs -g
```

Since version 3.4, the `mocha-phantomjs` module uses PhantomJS as a peer dependency, which means that we do not have to install the browser manually.

After successful installation, we are ready to run our test. The command that we have to type in our console is `mocha-phantomjs http://localhost:9000\?test=1`. There are back slashes because otherwise, if this wasn't the case, the terminal may not have interpreted the line correctly.

The result is shown in the following screenshot:

```
krasimir$ mocha-phantomjs http://localhost:9000\?test=1                    1 ↵


  Testing
    ✓ Test case



  1 passing (5ms)
```

This is pretty much the same result that we got in the browser. The good thing is that the process now happens in the terminal.

Testing user registration

Let's use the setup built in the previous sections and write an actual test. Let's say that we want to make sure that our registering page works. The following are the two processes that we want to capture with our test:

- Filling the form with wrong data and making sure that the application shows an error message
- Filling the form with correct data and seeing a successful message

We are going to use PhantomJS as our headless (virtual) browser. So, all we have to do is load our registration page and simulate user interactions, such as typing in the fields and pressing the buttons.

Simulating user interaction

There are a couple of issues that we are going to resolve. The first one is the actual simulation of user actions. From a JavaScript point of view, these actions are translated to events dispatched by some particular DOM elements. The following helper method will become a part of the `tests/spec.js` file:

```
describe("Testing", function () {

  var trigger = function(element, event, eventGroup, keyCode) {
    var e = window.document.createEvent(eventGroup || 'MouseEvents');
    if(keyCode) {
      e.keyCode = e.which = keyCode;
    }
    e.initEvent(event, true, true);
    return element.dispatchEvent(e);
  }

  it("Registration", function (done) {
    // ... our test here
  });

});
```

The `trigger` function accepts an element, the name of an event, an event group, and a key code. The first two arguments are mandatory. The third one has a default value of `MouseEvents` and the last one is optional. We are going to use the method to trigger the `change` and `click` events.

Filling and submitting the registration form

Let's start by filling the input fields of our registration form. It is worth mentioning that the code that we are going to write runs in a browser so that we have access to `document.querySelector`, for example. The following lines type a string in the first name field:

```
var firstName = document.querySelector('#first-name');
firstName.value = 'First name';
trigger(firstName, 'change');
```

Sending a string to the `firstName` element updates the user interface. However Ractive.js, our client-side framework, does not know about this change. The dispatching of the `change` event solves this problem.

We will use the same pattern to add values to the last name, e-mail, and password fields:

```
var lastName = document.querySelector('#last-name');
lastName.value = 'Last name';
trigger(lastName, 'change');

var email = document.querySelector('#email');
email.value = 'wrong email';
trigger(email, 'change');

var password = document.querySelector('#password');
password.value = 'password';
trigger(password, 'change');
```

The value of the e-mail's input field is invalid. This is done on purpose. We want to capture the case where the backend returns an error. To finish the operation, we have to click on the **register** button:

```
trigger(document.querySelector('input[value="register"]'),
  'click');
```

If we run the test now, we will see the following screenshot:

```
Testing
  1) Registration


0 passing (2s)
1 failing

1) Testing Registration:
   timeout of 2000ms exceeded
```

The test basically fails with a timeout. This is because we didn't call the done function. However, even then, we do not have any assertions.

Now, things get interesting. The processes that occur in the browser are asynchronous. This means that we cannot simply run our assertion after we click the button. We should wait for a while. The usage of setTimeout is not acceptable in these cases. The right approach here is to tweak the code of the application so that it notifies the outside world that a particular job is done. In our case, this is the submission of the registration form. To be more precise, we have to update s/controllers/Register.js:

```
module.exports = Ractive.extend({
  template: require('../../tpl/register'),
  components: {
    navigation: require('../views/Navigation'),
    appfooter: require('../views/Footer')
  },
  onrender: function() {
    ...
    this.on('register', function() {
      userModel.create(function(error, result) {
        ...
        self.fire('form-submitted');
      });
    });
  }
});
```

The addition is `self.fire('form-submitted')`. Once the model returns the response and we process it, we dispatch an event. For the users who visit the site, this line does nothing. However, for our test suite, this is a way to find out when the backend responds and the user interface is updated. This is when we have to make our assertions.

Tweaking the code's execution order

The dispatching of the event is nice, but it does not solve the problem entirely. We need to reach the `Register` controller and subscribe to the `form-submitted` message. In our test, we have access to the global scope (the `window` object). Let's use it as a bridge and provide a shortcut to the currently used controller, as follows:

```
// frontend/js/app.js
var showPage = function(newPage) {
  if(currentPage) currentPage.teardown();
  currentPage = newPage;
  body.innerHTML = '';
  currentPage.render(body);
  currentPage.on('navigation.goto', function(e, route) {
    Router.navigate(route);
  });
  window.currentPage = currentPage;
  if(typeof window.onAppReady !== 'undefined') {
    window.onAppReady();
  }
}
```

In the `app.js` file, we switched the pages of our application. This is the perfect place for our tweak because at this point, we know which controller is rendered.

One last thing that you should do before continuing with the actual test is to make sure that your social network is fully initialized and there is a view that is being rendered. This again needs access to the global `window` object. Our test will store a function in the `window.onAppReady` property, and the application will run it when PhantomJS opens the page. Note that attaching objects or variables to the global scope is not considered a good practice. However, in order to make our test work, we need such little tricks. We can always skip this while compiling a file for production release.

In `backend/tpl/pageTest.html`, we have the following code:

```
<script src="/socket.io/socket.io.js"></script>
<script src="/static/js/ractive.js"></script>
<script src="/static/js/app.js"></script>
```

```
<div id="mocha"></div>
<script src="/node_modules/mocha/mocha.js"></script>
<script src="/node_modules/chai/chai.js"></script>
<script>
  mocha.ui('bdd');
  mocha.reporter('html');
  expect = chai.expect;
</script>
<script src="/tests/spec.js"></script>
<script>
  if (window.mochaPhantomJS) { mochaPhantomJS.run(); }
  else { mocha.run(); }
</script>
```

If we continue using these lines, our test will fail because no UI is rendered when our assertions are executed. Instead, we should use the new `onAppReady` property to delay the calling of the `run` method in the following way:

```
<div id="mocha"></div>
<script src="/node_modules/mocha/mocha.js"></script>
<script src="/node_modules/chai/chai.js"></script>
<script>
  mocha.ui('bdd');
  mocha.reporter('html');
  expect = chai.expect;
</script>
<script src="/tests/spec.js"></script>
<script>
  window.onAppReady = function() {
    if (window.mochaPhantomJS) { mochaPhantomJS.run(); }
    else { mocha.run(); }
  }
</script>
<script src="/socket.io/socket.io.js"></script>
<script src="/static/js/ractive.js"></script>
<script src="/static/js/app.js"></script>
```

Thus, we included Mocha and Chai. We configured the testing framework, added a function that will be executed when `onAppReady` is called, and then we ran the actual application.

Listening to the form-submitted event

The very last code that we have to write is to subscribe for the `form-submitted` event, which is dispatched by our controller when the form is submitted and the result of the backend is processed. Our API should first respond with an error because we set a wrong e-mail value (`email.value = 'wrong email'`). Here is how we capture the error message:

```
var password = document.querySelector('#password');
password.value = 'password';
trigger(password, 'change');

window.currentPage.on('form-submitted', function() {
  var error = document.querySelector('.error');
  expect(!!error).to.be.equal(true);
  done();
});

trigger(document.querySelector('input[value="register"]'),
  'click');
```

The `!!error` item cast the error variable to a Boolean. We will check for the existence of the error element. If it is there, then the test passes. The result in the console is as follows:

```
krasimir$ mocha-phantomjs http://localhost:9000/register\?test\=1


Testing
  ✓ Registration


1 passing (39ms)
```

We verified the error reporting. Let's close the cycle by making sure that the successful message appears when all the fields are filled properly:

```
var submitted = 0;
window.currentPage.on('form-submitted', function() {
  if(submitted === 0) {
    submitted++;
    var error = document.querySelector('.error');
    expect(!!error).to.be.equal(true);
    var email = document.querySelector('#email');
```

```
        var validEmail = 'test' + (new Date()).getTime() +
          '@test.com';
        email.value = validEmail;
        trigger(email, 'change');
        trigger(document.querySelector('input[value="register"]'),
          'click');
      } else {
        var success = document.querySelector('.success');
        expect(!!success).to.be.equal(true);
        done();
      }
    });
```

The `form-submitted` event will be dispatched twice. So, we will use an additional `submitted` variable to distinguish between both the calls. In the first case, we will check for `.error`, while in the second one, we will check for `.success`. After running the `mocha-phantomjs` command, we will get the same result as before, but this time, we are sure that the entire registration process works. Note that we attach a dynamically generated timestamp so that we get different e-mails every time.

Testing with DalekJS

DalekJS is an open source UI testing tool that is written entirely in JavaScript. It acts as a test runner. It has its own API to perform user interface interactions. A very interesting feature of DalekJS is that it works with different browsers. It is capable of running tests in PhantomJS and popular browsers such as Chrome, Safari, Firefox, and Internet Explorer. It uses a **WebDriver JSON-Wire** protocol to communicate with these browsers and basically control what goes on in them.

Installing DalekJS

First, we need to install DalekJS's command-line tool. It is distributed as a Node.js package. So, the following command will download the necessary files:

```
npm install dalek-cli -g
```

When the process finishes, we can run the `dalek` command in our terminal. The next step is to add the `dalekjs` module in our dependencies. This is the package that summons the tool's API. So, two more lines are needed in the `package.json` file:

```
{
  ...
  "dependencies": {
    "dalekjs": "0.0.9",
```

```
        "dalek-browser-chrome": "0.0.11"
        ...
    }
}
```

We mentioned that DalekJS works with real browsers such as Chrome, Safari, and Firefox. There are dedicated packages that deal with all of these browsers. For example, if we want to test in the Chrome browser, we have to install `dalek-browser-chrome` as the dependency.

Using the DalekJS API

DalekJS works in a similar way to the `mocha-phantomjs` module. We write our test in a file and simply pass that file to a command in our terminal. Let's create a new file called `tests/dalekjs.spec.js` and put the following code inside it:

```
module.exports = {
  'Testing registration': function (test) {
    test
    .open('http://localhost:9000/register')
    .setValue('#first-name', 'First name')
    .setValue('#last-name', 'Last name')
    .setValue('#email', 'wrong email')
    .setValue('#password', 'password')
    .click('input[value="register"]')
    .waitForElement('.error')
    .assert.text('.error').to.contain('Invalid or missing email')
    .setValue('#email', 'test' + (new Date()).getTime() +
      '@test.com')
    .click('input[value="register"]')
    .waitForElement('.success')
    .assert.text('.success').to.contain('Registration successful')
    .done();
  }
};
```

The tool requires that we export an object, the keys of which are our test cases. We have only one case called `Testing registration`. We pass a function that receives a `test` argument, which gives us access to the DalekJS API.

The API of the module is designed in such a way that it is quite easy to understand what is going on. We open a specific URL and set values to the input fields. Like in the previous test, we will type in a wrong e-mail value and press the **Submit** button. The `.waitForElement` method is handy here because the operation is asynchronous. Once we detect the existence of the `.error` element, we will continue by writing the correct e-mail value and submitting the form again.

To run the test, we have to type `dalek ./tests/dalekjs.spec.js -b chrome` in the console. DalekJS will open a real Chrome window, which will execute the test and report the following in the terminal:

```
krasimir$ dalek ./tests/dalekjs.spec.js -b chrome
Running tests
Running Browser: Google Chrome
OS: Mac OS X 10.10.2 x86_64
Browser Version: 40.0.2214.115

RUNNING TEST - "Testing registration"
▶ OPEN http://localhost:9000/register
▶ SETVALUE #first-name
▶ SETVALUE #last-name
▶ SETVALUE #email
▶ SETVALUE #password
▶ CLICK input[value="register"]
▶ WAITFORELEMENT
✔ TEXT
▶ SETVALUE #email
▶ CLICK input[value="register"]
▶ WAITFORELEMENT
✔ TEXT
✔ 2 Assertions run
✔ TEST - "Testing registration" SUCCEEDED

2/2 assertions passed. Elapsed Time: 2.54 sec
```

With DalekJS, we did not have to tweak our application's code. There is no additional assertion library or testing framework. All this is wrapped in a single module that is easy to use and install.

From another point of view, DalekJS may not be useful to every project. For example, it may not be useful when we need to interact with the code of the application or if we need something that is not listed in the provided API.

Summary

In this chapter, we saw how to test our user interface. We successfully solved a couple of issues and used tools such as Mocha, Chai, and DalekJS. Testing our code is important, but it is often not enough. Tests that simulate user interaction and prove that our software works properly should exist.

Index

DalekJS API
  using 192, 193
database
  content, storing 109, 110
  record, creating 126-128
database server
  MongoDB, connecting to 71
date property 110
directory structure 52

E

emit function 12
entry point
  constructing, of application 61, 62
event loop library
  URL 2
events
  managing, to particular page 137-140
  working with 11, 12
execution order, code
  tweaking 188, 189

F

feed, user
  displaying 110-113
files
  posting 114-119
  reading 11
  saving, with Node.js 33-36
  writing 11
form
  adding, for creating pages 124, 125
  adding, to post text messages 105, 106
  filling 186-188
  submitting 186-188
form-submitted event
  listening to 190
friends
  fetching, from database 97-99
  finding 91
  model, writing 94-96

search page, adding 91-94
selecting 141, 142
users, making as 99-101

G

Grunt 19-22
Gulp
  about 22-24, 39
  concatenating with 39, 40

H

headless browser 184
HTML5 history API
  reference link 58
HTML templates
  defining, in script tags 45, 46
  delivering 45
  HTML, writing inside JavaScript 46, 47
  loading externally 46
  precompiling 47, 48

I

IDs, friends
  sending, to backend 141, 142

J

Jasmine 178
JavaScript files
  app.js 54
  ractive.js 54

L

Less
  about 37
  URL 37
linked users
  displaying, on Profile page 102-104
loading keyword 93

V

V8

URL 2

views

managing 64, 65

W

WebSockets

about 157, 158

Ajax long-polling 158

Ajax polling 158

benefits 157, 158

defining 157, 158

HTML5 Server-sent

Events (EventSource) 158

HTTP communication 157

used, for real-time web apps 157

Thank you for buying
Node.js By Example

About Packt Publishing

Packt, pronounced 'packed', published its first book, *Mastering phpMyAdmin for Effective MySQL Management*, in April 2004, and subsequently continued to specialize in publishing highly focused books on specific technologies and solutions.

Our books and publications share the experiences of your fellow IT professionals in adapting and customizing today's systems, applications, and frameworks. Our solution-based books give you the knowledge and power to customize the software and technologies you're using to get the job done. Packt books are more specific and less general than the IT books you have seen in the past. Our unique business model allows us to bring you more focused information, giving you more of what you need to know, and less of what you don't.

Packt is a modern yet unique publishing company that focuses on producing quality, cutting-edge books for communities of developers, administrators, and newbies alike. For more information, please visit our website at www.packtpub.com.

About Packt Open Source

In 2010, Packt launched two new brands, Packt Open Source and Packt Enterprise, in order to continue its focus on specialization. This book is part of the Packt Open Source brand, home to books published on software built around open source licenses, and offering information to anybody from advanced developers to budding web designers. The Open Source brand also runs Packt's Open Source Royalty Scheme, by which Packt gives a royalty to each open source project about whose software a book is sold.

Writing for Packt

We welcome all inquiries from people who are interested in authoring. Book proposals should be sent to author@packtpub.com. If your book idea is still at an early stage and you would like to discuss it first before writing a formal book proposal, then please contact us; one of our commissioning editors will get in touch with you.

We're not just looking for published authors; if you have strong technical skills but no writing experience, our experienced editors can help you develop a writing career, or simply get some additional reward for your expertise.

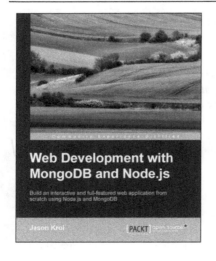

Using Node.js for UI Testing

ISBN: 978-1-78216-052-6   Paperback: 146 pages

Learn how to easily automate testing of your web apps using Node.js, Zombie.js and Mocha

1. Use automated tests to keep your web app rock solid and bug-free while you code.

2. Use a headless browser to quickly test your web application every time you make a small change to it.

3. Use Mocha to describe and test the capabilities of your web app.

Building Scalable Apps with Redis and Node.js

ISBN: 978-1-78398-448-0   Paperback: 316 pages

Develop customized, scalable web apps through the integration of powerful Node.js frameworks

1. Design a simple application and turn it into the next Instagram.

2. Integrate utilities such as Redis, Socket.io, and Backbone to create Node.js web applications.

3. Learn to develop a complete web application right from the frontend to the backend in a streamlined manner.

Please check **www.PacktPub.com** for information on our titles